SLAVERY

IN THE

UNITED STATES OF AMERICA;

ITS NATIONAL RECOGNITION AND RELATIONS,

FROM THE

ESTABLISHMENT OF THE CONFEDERACY,

TO THE

PRESENT TIME.

A WORD TO THE NORTH AND THE SOUTH.

BY HENRY SHERMAN,

COUNSELLOR AT LAW.

—"Then I thought that Conciliators were but ignorant men, that were willing to please all, and would pretend to reconcile the world by principles which they did not understand themselves; I have since perceived, that if the amiableness of peace and concord had no hand in the business, yet greater light, and stronger judgment, usually are with the Reconcilers, than with either of the contending parties."—RICHARD BAXTER'S *review of his early opinions.*

SECOND EDITION.

HARTFORD:
HURLBURT & POND, PUBLISHERS.
1860.

CASE, LOCKWOOD AND COMPANY, PRINTERS.

TO

THE FRIENDS OF

THE SUPREMACY OF OUR NATIONAL SOVEREIGNTY,

AND

OUR NATIONAL SOVEREIGNTY IN ITS SUPREMACY,

THE

TRUE FRIENDS OF

THE UNION, OF FREEDOM, AND HUMANITY,

THIS VOLUME

IS FRATERNALLY INSCRIBED BY

THE AUTHOR.

PREFACE

I HAVE long thought that the more modern controversies on the subject of Slavery, which have obtained in this country, have originated mostly in the absence of a just and proper understanding and appreciation of the Theory of our Government in its National, State, and Territorial relations, under the Constitution, and the changes which these have undergone by the extension of our National domain and jurisdiction beyond the anticipations and calculations of its framers. In preparing this work for the press, I have endeavored to develope these relations and changes in their complicity with this agitating topic, with a view to a more general understanding of it, and a more harmonious acquiesence in the privileges, as well as the restraints, of which it has been made the subject.

The Earl of Chatham, standing in his place in the British House of Lords to oppose the aggressions of Ministry upon the rights of the American Colonies, in 1775, made the memorable and truthful declaration—"In every free State it is the Constitution, and the Constitution only, which limits both Sovereignty and Allegiance. This doctrine is no temporary doctrine taken up on particular occasions, to answer particular purposes. It is involved in no metaphysical doubts and intricacies, but is clear, precise, and determinate. It is recorded in all our Law books. It is written in the great Volume of Nature."

In this country, there are those who say with General Walker, in his letter of resignation, addressed to Secretary Cass,—" The Constitution is not Sovereign because it is created by Sovereignty. With us Sovereignty rests exclusively with the people of each State.—The National Government is not Sovereign, much less any department of that Government, for the same reason."

And again, there are those whose views are expressed by General Lane, in a letter from the Territory of Kansas, January, 1858, wherein he says—" I suppose you know that the feeling here is strong against any Congressional Enabling Act. We want no interference with our affairs by Congress; feeling that we are fully competent to settle these matters ourselves. We want to be let alone."

And again, there are others still, who cherish the sentiment of Lord Chatham. Now, exclusively of all partizan feeling on the subject, it is evident that the doctrine enunciated by the latter, is directly at variance with that maintained by either of the other class of thinkers. Yet it contains that great principle of freedom, the violation of which caused the Revolution of 1688, in England, whose results were the overthrow of the doctrine of the Divine Right of Kings, the recognition of the people as a source of Sovereignty in the State, and the establishment of the Crown on the heads, and the succession in the line, of

William and Mary, Prince and Princess of Orange, by act of Parliament, by Law, in 1690. In other words, it gave birth to the Free Constitution of Great Britain, to which the Earl of Chatham refers.

Just one century after this, the American Revolution inaugurated the greater triumph of the same principle of Freedom, in the establishment of a freer Government and Sovereignty, called the United States of America, under a freer Constitution, which was finally ratified by all of the States in 1790.

Both of these Constitutions were founded upon the principle that there can be no allegiance where there is no Sovereignty. And that where there is Sovereignty, there must of necessity be allegiance. If then " with us, Sovereignty rests exclusively with the people of each State," where rests allegiance? Does the State owe allegiance to the people, or do the people owe allegiance to the State? Do the people owe allegiance to the Constitution, or the Constitution to the people? Or do the people, in their exclusive Sovereignty, owe allegiance only to themselves?

With us, there is a National Sovereignty, and there is also a State Sovereignty. There are State Constitutions which limit both Sovereignty and Allegiance in the State; And there is a National Constitution which limits both Sovereignty and Allegiance in the United States. Each has its particular, appropriate, and necessary sphere of action. Either may claim and enforce the particular, appropriate, and necessary Allegiance which is its due. With us there are no Territorial Constitutions.

Allegiance in a State, is submission to the Supreme

power of the State within the limits of its jurisdiction. Allegiance in a Nation composed of Confederated States, and dependent Territories, is submission to the Supreme power of the National Sovereignty within the sphere of its jurisdiction. In either case, both Sovereignty and Allegiance are limited by the Constitution, and by *the Constitution only.* In either case, it is not for the people to disclaim or withold their allegiance because, perchance, they were parties to the Compact which limits and defines the Sovereignty. With us, even the States in their Sovereign capacity owe a certain allegiance to the National Supremacy, which allegiance is also limited by the Constitution. It is not in the power, therefore, of the people of a single State to throw off the allegiance due from the State to the National Sovereignty, without destroying the Sovereignty of the State itself. Nor is it in the power of the people of any one of the States to throw off their allegiance to its Sovereignty without abrogating the State Constitution. With us, so far is Sovereignty from resting "exclusively with the people of each State," so restrained are they by the National Sovereignty, that they cannot change their own State Government from a Republican to a Monarchical, or to any other form. Hence it is absurd, nay more it is revolutionary, to say that *because* the people united in creating the National Sovereignty, *therefore it is not Sovereign.*

Much less are the people Sovereign in the Territory, or Territories, belonging to the National Sovereignty, called the United States. The very idea of ownership involves the idea of Sovereign jurisdiction, which also includes the idea of allegiance. This Sovereignty and allegiance may indeed be qualified, or limited, by an enactment of the General Sovereignty establishing a local Territorial Government, but neither is thereby extinguished, nor is the authority thereby delegated to the people, or to the Territorial Government, made exclusive: Nor does it give the people inhabiting therein a right to a higher state of political existence. The transfer from a Territorial to a State Organization involves a declaration of independence on the part of the Territory, or a relinquishment of its Supremacy over it on the part of the National Sovereignty. It proposes a condition of political existence which cannot be created without depriving the National Sovereignty of a part at least of its Supremacy. Not only so, but, with us, it also places the New Organization in the relations and position of a co-partner in the Sovereignty existing in the National Confederacy.

And has the National Sovereignty no interest in this political transformation? May it not say whether at all, or upon what terms, or subject to what conditions, it will consent to this new creation? Consent to relinquish its own Supremacy over its own Territory? And admit the New State, thus created, into the great Federal Copartnership?

The People of the United States, the source of Sovereignty with us, have said, CONSTITUTION, ARTICLE VI., SEC. 2,—This Constitution, and the laws of the United States *which shall be made in pursuance thereof*, and all Treaties made, or which shall be made *under the authority* of the United States, shall be the Supreme Law of the land: and the Judges *of every State*, shall be bound thereby, anything in *the Constitution and laws of any State*, to the contrary notwithstanding."

We may look in vain for a better exposition of Sovereignty in the Government of the United States than is here found. Supremacy to govern is Sovereignty. The Constitution is not Sovereignty, it is the Charter of Sovereignty. It is not law except in the sense of its Supremacy. Nor yet is it Supreme by itself alone, but also in the laws *made in pursuance of* its provisions, and in the Treaties made *under the authority* which it establishes. Law is not the act, but the voice of Sovereignty. The Constitution does not act; the Law does not act; Treaties do not act; but it is the Officers of the Government in their various departments who perform its behests. They act, and act with all the power and might of the Sovereignty whose laws they enforce, whose mandates they execute, whose voice directs their duties. It is immaterial how this Supreme power originates, or how it exists, so long as it is legitimate. While it exists, its powers are Sovereign within the sphere of its jurisdiction. This is limited *by the Constitution only*, and cannot be infringed or repudiated, either by the States, or by the people of the States, or Territories, so long as the Constitution is maintained in its integrity.

The Sovereignty of the Crown of Great Britain, established under the English Constitution by the Revolution of 1688, was called a Popular Sovereignty, not because it recognized the Supremacy of the popular will, but because it conceded that *the people were one of the sources of* its

Sovereignty. The Constitution of the United States established a freer and still more Popular Sovereignty, in that it recognized the People *as the only source of its Supremacy.* Popular Sovereignty does not mean the "exclusive Sovereignty of the People;" or a Sovereignty exclusive of Constitutions and Laws; but a Sovereignty, whether State or National, established under a Constitution formed by the people, acting freely, and without any extraneous or arbitrary compulsion or restraint. The Constitution thus established by the people is the Charter of Supremacy to the government, in every Popular Sovereignty. A State Sovereignty is called a Popular Sovereignty because in it both Sovereignty and Allegiance are limited by a Constitution created by the free voice of the people. So also is the National Sovereignty of the United States called a Popular Sovereignty, for the same reason. A Popular Territorial Sovereignty is an absurdity. The very terms are contradictory and antagonistic. Territorial is colonial; it implies dependence, and sovereign dependence is a political absurdity.

The people inhabiting in a dependent Territory, therefore, must necessarily be subject to the Sovereignty upon which they depend. The Sovereignty acquired under the Constitution is supreme. The Sovereignty acquired by the cession of Territory is supreme. The Sovereignty acquired by the purchase of Territory is also supreme; and if there be any greater supremacy in Sovereignty, it certainly must be that title to supremacy which is acquired by conquest. In all these modes of acquisition the exclusive supremacy of the National Government in its Territorial domain, thus expanded, cannot be questioned. It is above and beyond all doubt and peradventure. And although, with us, by general consent as well as by special compact, the Constitution has been adopted and referred to as limiting the exercise of thisSupremacy in our Federal and State relations, still the Supremacy of the National Sovereignty in its own Territorial domain is not thereby depreciated or destroyed. It may indeed delegate a portion of its authority to the people, by the establishment of a local Territorial government, but it does not thereby relinquish its own Supremacy, or release the people inhabiting therêin from their allegiance to it, or render them independent of its superior Sovereignty. It may, at will, repeal the Act conferring those powers, and resume its exclusive jurisdiction over them. Hence there is, there can be, no inherent right in the people inhabiting in such Territory to form a government for themselves, independently of the National Sovereignty. This right, with us, is *exclusive* only in the people of a State, *provided* it be Republican and in conformity with their allegiance to the National Sovereignty. The great error of our day is, in claiming that *State rights* belong to the people inhabiting in the Territories *before they become a State.* With us, they cannot become a State Organization without the consent of the Sovereignty on which they depend. They cannot adopt a Constitution for their own government, in anticipation of their transfer from a Territorial to a State Organization, which would be of any validity, or worth, without the assent of the National Sovereignty, or its recognition of it after it is made. Still if the Supreme

Sovereignty does consent to their transition from a Territorial to a State Organization, it must necessarily consent, nay more it guarantees, that the New Government shall be a Popular one; that is, a Government, or Sovereignty, established under a Constitution framed and adopted by the people who are to be ruled under it, acting freely, and without any hostile compulsion, hindrance, or restraint whatsoever. Any other theory than this would be fatal to the preservation of this Union, without any reference to the question of Slavery.

Thus much I have ventured by way of Preface or introduction to this work, although I may make some repetition of what I have here said in treating of these principles in their bearing upon Slavery in the United States. The whole subject is one which ought to be more carefully pondered over, and clearly understood, by our statesmen and politicians of the present day, as well as by the people in all parts of the country: And if I may hereby contribute towards its elucidation in any degree I shall not regret having attempted it.

HENRY SHERMAN.

HARTFORD, CT., Nov. 1st, 1858.

CONTENTS.

CHAPTER I.

SLAVERY UNDER THE CONSTITUTION.

INTRODUCTION—Slavery in the Original States—The Declaration of Independence—The Confederation—The Ordinance of 1787—The Constitution—The Compact of the Confederation and Slavery—The Ordinance of 1787 and Slavery—The Ordinance of 1787 and the Constitution—The Constitution and Slavery—The Constitution, the Ordinance of 1787, and Slavery—The Protective Law of 1793—The Constitution and the Protective Law of 1793—The Constitution, the Protective Law of 1793, and Slavery—The Constitution and the admission of New States—The Constitutional theory of the recognition of Slavery—Restrictive Acts of Congress from 1794 to 1820—The purchase of the Louisiana Territory—Its relations to Slavery—Act distributing the Territory—Its restrictions upon Slavery—The Convention with France and Slavery in said Territory—Character of the Compact—Act of 1805 in relation to said Territory—The Admission of the State of Louisiana—Organization of the Missouri Territory—Admission of Mississippi—Alabama—Ohio—Indiana—Illinois, and Slavery—The Admission of Louisiana and Slavery—Extent of the Constitutional recognition of Slavery: page 9.

CHAPTER II.

SLAVERY OUTSIDE OF THE CONSTITUTION.

Sovereignty under the Confederation—Sovereignty under the Constitution—The Constitutional National Sovereignty—Recognition of Slavery under the Constitution—The National Sovereignty outside of the Constitution—Source of its Supremacy over the New Territory—Admission of New States by it—Its power over Slavery—Application of Missouri for admission into the Union—Nature of the application—Its history—The Compact for her admission—Its unconstitutionality—Its nature and relations to Slavery—The resolution of admission—The Annexation and admission of Texas—Nature of the Compact—Its unconstitutionality—Its relations to Slavery—The acquisition of foreign Territory from Mexico—Its relations to Slavery—The Compromise Measures of 1850—Their nature and relations to Slavery—The Protective Law of 1850: . . . . page 61.

CHAPTER III.

THE REPEAL OF THE MISSOURI COMPACT.

Character of the National Sovereignty of the United States on the admission of Missouri—The Compact with Missouri—Its repeal—The effect upon Slavery—Opinion of the Supreme Court in the Dred Scott Case—Its relations to Slavery—Rule laid down for the construction of the Constitution—Its general applicability—Its relation to the powers of Congress in the New Territory—In the admission of New States formed out of it—Over Slavery in said Territory and New States—Effect of the Repeal of the Missouri Compact in 1854—The enforcement of the Protective Law of 1850—Effect of the Repeal and the Opinion of the Supreme Court upon Slavery—Nature of the Compromise Compacts—Their importance to Slavery—Reasons for the Repeal of the Missouri Compact applicable to the Compact with Texas—To the Compromise Measures of 1850—So also of the ruling of the Supreme Court—Source of the Supremacy of the Government over the New Territory defined by it—This Supremacy the basis of the Compromises in relation to Slavery—The Compromises the only reliance of Slavery—Importance of good faith in their observance—The further extension and recognition of Slavery—The necessity of concession and conciliation—The Common National standpoint—Paramount importance of the Union to the cause of freedom and humanity—Conclusion: . . . . . . page 140.

SLAVERY IN THE UNITED STATES,

ITS

NATIONAL RECOGNITION AND RELATIONS,

FROM THE ESTABLISHMENT OF THE CONFEDERACY TO THE PRESENT TIME.

CHAPTER I.

SLAVERY UNDER THE CONSTITUTION.

I.

THERE is, perhaps, no subject which presents itself to the consideration of every citizen of our Republic, at the present day, with more especial interest than the subject of African or Negro Slavery. And there is none which, in its national aspects and relations, is, generally, so little understood. If, as in the original States, its recognition and extension were restricted to the natural increase of an existing slave population as the only source of supply, it could not create any material apprehension. But the extension of our national domain and sovereignty beyond its original constitutional limit, by the acquisition of foreign territory, and its liability to be in like manner still farther extended, thus introducing continually within our national jurisdiction an additional slave population, with its additional source of increase, make it a matter of great and increasing national interest and importance to us all. It is, therefore, essential and necessary that the common, and more especially the educated mind should be rightly informed in relation to it, and that the true theory and extent of its national recognition and relations should be clearly understood. I propose to consider the subject, in these aspects of it, under two general propositions embraced in the following interrogatories, viz.:—

First. HOW FAR IS SLAVERY AND THE OWNERSHIP OF SLAVE PROPERTY RECOGNIZED AND PROTECTED UNDER THE PROVISIONS OF THE CONSTITUTION?

Second. WHAT IS THE ORIGIN AND THE BASIS OF ITS RECOGNITION AND PROTECTION BEYOND THE CONSTITUTIONAL LIMIT?

These are questions which address themselves with peculiar force to every man who loves our national Union, who is proud of our national character, and who would preserve both in perpetual and happy harmony with the supremacy of the Federal sovereignty and the rights of the individual States; with the paramount law of the Constitution and the great interests and claims of freedom and humanity every where. I shall endeavor to answer them fairly, without fear or favor, without prejudice or partiality toward any portion of our country, and without any sectarian, sectional, or partisan aim or bias. I shall treat them as political questions merely, without any reference to Slavery as a question of morals, or of religion, and without expressing or meaning to intimate any opinion as to the right or the wrong of holding human beings in bondage.

I premise, then, that THE DECLARATION OF INDEPENDENCE was a political manifesto enunciating certain political rights, claimed to be inherent in the American Colonies of Great Britain under the British Constitution, of which they were wrongfully deprived by the government of the parent State, the deprivation of which justified them in breaking away from their allegiance to it and proclaiming themselves independent of its sovereignty. It was a compact under and by virtue of which the Colonies mutually pledged themselves, each to every other, to assume a position of independence before the world, to maintain it at all hazards, and to abide by it forever.

This compact was revolutionary in its origin, its nature, and its aims, and had no specific reference to any other than the revolutionary circumstances which originated and followed it. It was made more specific and permanent by the *Compact of the Confederation* under which the Colonies leagued together *in a perpetual union*, achieved their independence, and became *as United States* a sovereign power on earth.

Whatever may have been the political guarantees, pledges, or stipulations, embraced in the Declaration of Independence, these were superseded by, except so far as they were merged or comprehended in, *the Compact of the Confederation.* The latter was again qualified by the political compact contained in *the Ordinance of* 1787, *and wholly superseded* by the final compact of *the Constitution.*

The Ordinance of 1787 was a compact in relation to the proprietorship and government of certain territory, originally claimed to belong to individual States, and which, for the purpose of securing a more permanent national union, was by them ceded to the United States, for the common benefit of such States as should become members of the Federal Alliance proposed by the revolutionary Congress in the Articles of Confederation.

The Constitution was a compact between the people of the original States *for the establishment of their national unity under a General Sovereignty*, with specified powers, securing to the people in general and to the States in severalty, all the rights, privileges, and immunities, which they had acquired in achieving their independence of the parent power. Among these was the conceded right of property in human flesh and bones, Slavery. Their situation in relation to it was peculiar, and although it was felt to be a strange inheritance yet it was the heritage of all of them, and was the only oppression which could not be renounced or removed with the renunciation of the sovereignty of Great Britain.

Neither was it, nor could it be made, a matter of reproach to any of them. It was an institution introduced into America by the parent State, and acquiesced in by the colonies themselves, in an age and at a period in their history when the traffic was pursued by all nations without any special sense of its enormity.

The Northern Colonies participated in it as well as and equally with the Southern Colonies. The navigation of the New England ports was largely employed on the African coast, and her commercial marine continually engaged in the transportation and shipment of slaves to the different American markets, by the aid of American capital. No stigma, therefore, can be cast on our brethren in the South for its introduction, or for the fruits of its inheritance, which is not in like manner and equally applicable to us at the North, and to the English nation.* After its introduction all became equally eager to embark in the traffic, to avail themselves of its profits, and to cherish and protect the right of property which it gave in the subjects of their enterprise and their speculations. Hence the existence of Slavery and

* See Annals of Congress, 1791. App.

the ownership of slave property, were subjects which called for peculiar consideration, for indulgences and concessions, and for guards and guarantees, in the formation of a National Government which was to be of general, perpetual, and irrevocable jurisdiction.

THE COMPACT OF THE CONFEDERATION makes no mention of the subject of Slavery, and contains no specific provision in relation to it, although it is historically true that every one of the thirteen Original States which ratified it, was at the time a slaveholding State; and the CONFEDERATION was expressly designed to cement and make perpetual the league of union formed by the Colonies under the Declaration of Independence. The slightest approximation to the subject is found in the *Articles* of Confederation, which provide:—

ARTICLE IV. SEC. I.—"The better to secure and perpetuate mutual friendship and intercourse among the people of the different states in this union, the *free inhabitants* of each of these states,—paupers, vagabonds, and fugitives from justice excepted,—shall be entitled to all the privileges and immunities of *free citizens* in the several states; and the people of each state shall have free ingress and egress to and from any other state, and shall enjoy therein all the privileges of trade and commerce, subject to the same duties, impositions, and restrictions as the inhabitants thereof respectively: *provided* that such restrictions shall not extend so far as to prevent the removal of *property imported into any state* to any other state of which the owner is an inhabitant."

This latter clause was evidently intended to protect the ownership of slave property as well as ordinary merchandise, *in transitu* from the port of entry in one state to the place of ownership in another state.

But the first direct, general, and National recognition of Slavery and the right of property in negro slaves, of which we have any full record, is contained in the political compact made between the several states and the United States, for the government of the territory north-west of the river Ohio, commonly called THE ORDINANCE OF 1787, which provides,—

ARTICLE VI.—"There shall be neither slavery nor involuntary servitude *in the said territory*, otherwise than in the punishment of crimes, whereof the party shall have been duly convicted. *Provided always*, that any person escaping into the same, from whom labor or service is lawfully claimed *in any one of the original states*, such fugitive may be lawfully reclaimed and conveyed to the person claiming his or her labor or service as aforesaid."

The recital contained in the same Ordinance, and which precedes the articles of compact enumerated, of which the foregoing is one, declares:—"*It is hereby ordained and declared* by the authority aforesaid, that the following articles shall be considered *as articles of compact between the Original States and the people and states in the said territory*, and *forever remain unalterable* unless by the common consent."

It is evident that the phraseology here used is carefully selected, and was purposely guarded and specific. It is also evident that the compact was designed to be perpetual, and that it could be canceled or revoked only by the parties making it, acting in the same capacity and sustaining the same position and relations which they now occupied. It is apparent, too, that Slavery is here recognized as an existing institution, which conferred a right of property in the subjects of it, and which involved a right to reclaim the fugitive from its servitude. But at the same time it must be observed that this recognition of it is restrictive. It prohibits Slavery in general, while the provision for its protection is limited to *the said territory* as the place of refuge and recaption, and to *the Original States, or any one of them*, as the place of recognized ownership and escape. It could have no other application from the very terms of it. It could not have been intended to have any other, because it covered the whole domain, both state and national, included within the precincts of the Republic then called the United States. The person escaping must owe labor or service to *an inhabitant of one of the original states;* the service must be due *under the laws of the state* from which he is alleged to have escaped, and he can be reclaimed only when escaping *into the said territory.* The reverse of the provision could not be maintained. A person owned, perchance, *in the said territory*, or in any state formed out of the said territory, escaping into *any one of the original states*, could not be reclaimed under this provision. Nor could it reach the case of a fugitive from service due in *any one state*, escaping into *any other state.*

It is plain, then, that the Ordinance of 1787 recognized and protected, and was intended to recognize and protect, Slavery, or rather the ownership of slave property, only under the circumstances of ownership and escape specified. It is also evident that it did not then, and cannot now, of itself, give it protection beyond the specified limits, or under any other than the specified circumstances.

This Ordinance, I have observed, was made *a perpetual compact*, irrevocable except by the common consent of the respective parties to it. The parties were *the Original States*, (to whom *as United States* the said Territory had been ceded for the purposes of the Union,) on the one side; and *the people and States of the said Territory* on the other side. The pledge was mutual, reciprocal, and solemn, that Slavery should never be introduced there, and that it should never be recognized or protected there, except in the particular cases, and under the particular circumstances, and within the limits specified. This, too, whether the people inhabiting therein remained under a Territorial government, or were erected into a State and admitted into union with the Original States.

The agreement could not be varied, or canceled, nor could Slavery lawfully exist there as a local institution, without this common consent. Nor could it be recognized or protected elsewhere, *under this provision*, by the simple admission of other and then unknown members into the Confederacy, under any combination of circumstances not contemplated or provided for in the terms of the compact. New States or Territories, other than those composing *the Original Thirteen*, or any portion thereof, coming into the Confederacy thereafter, could not necessarily claim protection in the ownership of slave property, by virtue of the stipulation contained in this Ordinance.

Thus far was Slavery recognized, and the ownership of slave property protected, under the Confederation and the Ordinance of 1787. How was it under the Constitution?

II.

That the compact of the Constitution superseded the compact of the Confederation, in all respects, no one will deny. How did it affect the Ordinance of

1787? Did it revoke it? Did it extend or restrict, or vary in any way, its provisions? Let us see.

The same parties, *the original States*, which made the compact contained in the Ordinance, at a concurrent era also made the compact contained in the Constitution. If, therefore, the Constitution abrogated or varied, restricted or enlarged, the provisions of the Ordinance, it was done by *the common consent* referred to; and hence, whatever change was made, was equally binding on the original parties to either.

The recognition of Slavery by the Constitution is limited to three of its provisions. The first,—

ART. 1ST, *Sec. II.*, *Subd. 3d*, provides for the apportionment of direct taxes, and the ratio of representation in Congress, upon the slave population in the several States, in the proportion of three-fifths. Strictly speaking, however, this provision recognizes the existence of the slave population *as persons*, and not as property. Perhaps I am conceding too much, when I say it is a recognition of Slavery. I shall refer to it again, in connection with the subject, more particularly, hereafter. The second is,—

ART. I., *Sec. IX.*, *Subd.* 1, restricting the prohibitive powers of Congress over the importation of slaves, till after the year 1808, and this restriction is expressly limited to "*the States now existing*." But that provision in the Constitution which, it is generally conceded, more directly recognizes Slavery, and protects the ownership of slave property, reads thus:—

"ARTICLE IV., *Sec. 2d.* No person, held to service or labour *in one State*, under the laws thereof, *escaping into another*, shall, in consequence of any law or regulation therein, be discharged from such service or labour, but shall be delivered up on claim of the party to whom such service or labour may be due."

This provision is also restrictive in its terms. The protection given to Slavery is limited to *the several States*, as the places of ownership and escape as well as of refuge and reclamation. It does not comprehend persons escaping from any one State into any *Territory* of the United States, but into *another State*. If it was designed to abrogate the provision contained in the Ordinance of 1787, it, clearly, was not intended to protect the ownership of slave property in cases where the person escaped from any one State into any *Territory* of the United States. If it abrogated the Ordinance altogether, it most certainty took away the protective recognition guaranteed to Slavery *in the Territories*. Hence it would follow that *under the Constitution* there was no protective recognition given to the ownership of slave property when escaped into any of *the Territory* then belonging to the United States. This conclusion is inevitable, if it is claimed or conceded that the Constitution superseded the political compact contained in the Ordinance of 1787.

But let us look at it further in this connection. How far *was* the ownership of slave property intended to be recognized and protected by the Constitution, in the minds of its framers? To answer this question fully and fairly, we must determine what is meant by the terms *any one State* and *another State*. Have they a definite and specific reference, or an indefinite, illimitable application? This question, again, can be properly answered only by taking these words in connection with the Ordinance. The parties to the respective compacts have themselves made them correlative and supportive of each other. If the two co-exist, they must be taken to constitute but *one compact* in relation to the recognition of Slavery, or the ownership of slave property, in the State and Territorial domain of the United States. Do they co-exist, and *what is* the compact under them?

Now, that the Constitution was not intended to abrogate the Ordinance, and that it was the intention of its framers that the two should operate harmoniously, is evident from the following enactment of Congress, made immediately after its organization under the Constitution, entitled—

3

"*An Act to provide for the government of the Territory north-west of the river Ohio.*"

"Whereas, In order that the Ordinance of the United States in Congress assembled, for the government of the Territory north-west of the river Ohio, *may continue to have full effect*, it is requisite that certain provisions should be made *so as to adapt* the same *to the present Constitution* of the United States:—

"SECTION 1. *Be it enacted by the Senate and House of Representatives of the United States of America in Congress assembled*, That in all cases in which, by said Ordinance, any information is to be given or communication made, by the Governor of the said Territory, to the United States in Congress assembled, or to any of their officers, it shall be the duty of the said Governor to give such information, and to make such communication, to the President of the United States; and the President shall nominate, and, by and with the advice and consent of the Senate, shall appoint, all officers which by the said Ordinance were to have been appointed by the United States in Congress assembled, and all officers so appointed shall be commissioned by him; and in all cases where the United States in Congress assembled might, by the said Ordinance, revoke any commission, or remove from any office, the President is hereby declared to have the same powers of revocation and removal.

"SECTION 2. *And be it further enacted*, That in case of the death, removal, resignation, or necessary absence of the Governor of the said Territory, the Secretary thereof shall be, and he is hereby, authorized and required to execute all the powers and perform all the duties of the Governor during the vacancy occasioned by the removal, resignation, or necessary absence of the said Governor."

This enactment is conclusive on this point. No stronger demonstration can be given that there was no intention to abrogate the articles contained in the political compact of the Ordinance, or to change their force or validity. This Act, made for the avowed purpose of making that Ordinance conformable to the Constitution, with both of them before the national legislature, must be taken to have made every change that was necessary to accomplish that object. In all other respects the Ordinance was conceded not only, but declared, to be consistent and in harmony with the provisions of the Constitution. It was virtually thereby again decreed that it was to exist in perpetuity *as a political compact*, and should continue thereafter to be in full force, and have as full effect, as when originally made. Its provisions, its stipulations, its phraseology, were all declared, as it were, perfectly constitutional; and the Constitution was also declared to be in harmony with its provisions. The two were made co-existent, and supportive of each other.

Taking, then, the two provisions together,—the one in the sixth Article of the Ordinance, and the other in the fourth Article of the Constitution,—they limit and define the extent of the constitutional recognition of Slavery, or the ownership of slave property, which may be thus rendered:—"No person held to labor or service *in any one of the Original States*, under the laws thereof, escaping into *another of the Original States*, shall in consequence of any law or regulation therein, be discharged from such service or labor, but shall be delivered up on claim of the party to whom such service or labor may be due. And there shall be neither Slavery nor involuntary servitude in the said (north-west) Territory of the United States, otherwise than in the punishment of crimes whereof the party shall have been duly convicted: provided always, that any person escaping into the same (north-west territory) from whom labor or service is lawfully claimed *in any one of the Original States, such fugitive* may be lawfully reclaimed and conveyed to the person claiming his or her service as aforesaid."

I regard the words *the said Territory* and *the Original States* as clearly referring and restricting the provision to the then State and Territorial domain of the United States. They could not have any reference beyond this, because, to go beyond it was to go beyond the reach of the National domain, as well as the domain of the States, to exceed the National as well as the State jurisdictions. Hence it follows, that the utmost extent to which Slavery was recognized, and the power of Congress could be exercised to protect it *under the Constitution*, was limited to the thirteen Original States and the then Territorial precincts of the United States. Beyond that limit the Constitution did not intend to go, and did not, *because it could not.*

Again, the power of Congress to legislate on this subject under the Constitution is derived from ARTICLE I., *Section 8th, Subd.* 17, which provides,—

"The Congress shall have power to *make all laws* which shall be *necessary and proper* for carrying into execution the *foregoing* powers, and *all other* powers *vested by this Constitution in the government* of the United States, or *in any department or officer thereof.*"

The power to protect the ownership of slave property is not one of the enumerated "foregoing powers;" the latter part of this section, if any part of it, is the only source of the power in Congress to legislate on this subject, and hence its phraseology is important to be observed.

The first positive enactment of Congress under this provision in the Constitution is in the ACT OF

3*

FEBRUARY TWELFTH, 1793, called the Fugitive Slave Law, entitled "*An act respecting fugitives from justice, and persons escaping from the service of their masters*," which provides,—

"SECTION III. *And be it also enacted*, that when a person held to labor or service in any of the United States, or in either of the Territories *on the north-west or south* of the river Ohio, under the laws thereof, shall escape into *any other of the said States or Territory*, the person to whom such labor or service may be due, his agent or attorney, is hereby empowered to seize or arrest such fugitive from labor, and to take him or her before any judge of the circuit or district courts of the United States, residing or being within the state, or before any magistrate of a county, city, or town corporate, wherein such seizure or arrest shall be made, and upon proof to the satisfaction of such judge or magistrate, either by oral testimony, or affidavit taken before and certified by a magistrate of any such State or Territory, that the person so seized or arrested, doth, under the laws of the State *or Territory* from which he or she fled, owe service or labor to the person claiming him or her, it shall be the duty of such judge or magistrate to give a certificate thereof to such claimant, his agent or attorney, which shall be sufficient warrant for removing the said fugitive from labor, to the State *or Territory* from which he or she fled."

"SECTION IV. *And be it further enacted*, that any person who shall knowingly and willingly obstruct or hinder such claimant, his agent or attorney, in so seizing or arresting such fugitive from labor, or shall rescue such fugitive from such claimant, his agent or attorney, when so arrested pursuant to the authority herein given or declared, or shall harbor or conceal such person, after notice that he or she was a fugitive from labor, as aforesaid, shall, for either of the said offenses, forfeit and pay the sum of five hundred dollars, which penalty may be recovered by and for the benefit of such claimant, by action of debt, in any court proper to try the same; saving, moreover, to the person claiming such labor or service, the right of action for or on account of the said injuries, or either of them." (1 *United States Stat. at large*, 302.)

This Act, whatever its aim, could not have an operation inconsistent with the provisions of the Constitution, nor could it give recognition to Slavery, or protection to the ownership of slave property, beyond the limit of the then Territorial domain and sovereignty of the United States. It cannot, therefore, be construed as intended to protect it in places and under circumstances where, under the Constitutional provision, it could not be protected. Nor does it in terms (except as I shall presently notice) conflict with the construction which I have given to the Constitutional provision; nor had there been, saving the further cession of territory *south* of the river Ohio, for the common benefit, by others of the Original States, any enlargement of the territorial domain of the United States, previous to its passage, which would warrant us in giving it a more extended reference.

The phraseology of the act is, "*When a person,* held to labor *in any of the United States,* or in either of the Territories *on the north-west or south* of the river Ohio, under the laws thereof, shall escape *into any other of the said States or Territories,* the person to whom such service is due," &c. The same restrictive terms are here used as in the Ordinance of 1787, or referred to as defining and limiting the protective recognition of the law to the case of a person who is held *under an existing servitude* in any of the United States or in the Territory of the United States, and escaping into any other one of the same States, or specified Territory. The words *in any of the United States* clearly refer to the States then composing the Sovereignty called the United States. And the Territory intended to be covered by the provision is as clearly defined and specified by the words limiting it to the Territory then belonging to the United States, and described as lying *north-west and south of the river Ohio.* And the limitation is still farther restricted by the words, "escaping into *any other of the said states*, or (said) *territory*."

The slave property, therefore, the ownership of which was designed to be recognized and protected by this law of Congress, must be in a person owing service *in any one of the original States*, under the laws thereof, and escaping therefrom into any other of *the said Original States*, or into either of *the said* Territories. Or, (going beyond the constitutional provision,) of a person owing service in either of the said Territories, *under the laws thereof*, (in conflict with the Ordinance of 1787 as to the North-West Territory,) and escaping into any one of the said Original States, or into *the other of the said* Territories.

Allowing this act to be in strict conformity with the Constitution and the Ordinance of 1787, (which it evidently is not, of which hereafter,) we have here the full and only extent of the Constitutional power in Congress to recognize Slavery and to protect the ownership of slave property, by providing for and enforcing its reclamation. It can go no farther, not only because the very terms used to define its jurisdiction upon the subject limit it as to place and circumstances, but also because it comprehended the entire State and Territorial domain of the then United States. Beyond this, there was not and there could not have been, any claim or pretense that its jurisdiction extended, or was intended to reach, by any possible construction.

III.

Such was the nature and such was the utmost extent of the national recognition given to Slavery in the United States *under the Constitution.* The question of its recognition might well have been, and was, a question of National interest and importance, because it existed in every one of the then States. But it was merely the recognition of *an existing ownership* of slave property as to the *then existing States*, (see Constitution, Art. I., Sec. IX.,) although it might indeed include the ownership of all slave property imported into any one of them prior to the year 1808. But it was not a recognition of Slavery itself as a permanent National or State institution. It was a question of protection merely, and not a question of increase or extension. The question of its extension, if it had been at all seriously agitated, either in or out of Congress, in the legislatures or among the people of the States, was definitively settled by the political compact of the Ordinance of 1787; and lastingly so, it would seem, when that compact was made and declared to be in conformity with the Constitution.

If, however, the Constitution is to be regarded as having abrogated that compact, and taken to be the sole guide in its own construction on this subject, there can be no question but that the act of 1793 contravenes the constitutional provision for the reclamation of fugitives from service in two particulars, while it certainly is in conflict with the Ordinance of 1787.

First. It extends the right of reclamation of slave property over *Territory south* of the river Ohio, thereby embracing territory not a part of the national domain at the time of the adoption of the Constitution, and therefore not reached by the strict constitutional provision. And—

Second. It recognizes the ownership of slave property in the Territories *under the laws thereof*, and provides for its recaption when escaped *from any one such Territory* into any State, or *other such Territory* of the United States. In other words it makes *the Territories* referred to, both *north-west and south* of the river Ohio, places of recognized ownership and escape as well as places of refuge and reclamation, clearly in conflict with the very letter as well as the spirit of both the Ordinance and the Constitution.

But, it may be said, and it was undoubtedly so, that the law of 1793 was designed to protect the ownership of slave property in territory *south* of the river Ohio, which was a part of some of the southern States, original members of the Union, and which was by them ceded to the United States for the common benefit,—that slavery was already in existence there, and that the cession was made with the express reservation, or condition, that Congress should not pass any act of emancipation in reference thereto, but on the contrary should recognize and protect Slavery therein, in the same manner as if no cession had been made and as if the said Territory was still a part of the original State. I have no hesitation in conceding this to have been the compact of cession, and the act in question to have been made, in part, in pursuance of it. Still, the act was one of protection *in the existing ownership* of slave property, and not for the extension of Slavery. It still recognized and protected it only within the National or State domain, belonging to the original States in severalty, or as United States in common, *at the time of the adoption of the Constitution.*

The question, therefore, again recurs, how far does the act of 1793 constitutionally recognize and protect the ownership of slave property? Certainly it cannot go beyond the limit prescribed by the Constitution. In its very terms it is restricted to persons owing service or labor in any of *the said* United States, that is, in any one of the then existing or *Original* States. That is, the States which were parties to the original union under the Declaration of Independence, to the permanent union under the Confederation, and to the final compact of perpetual union under the Constitution. Their common union, their common trials, their common sacrifices, and their common labors, through all these transitions, were the basis of their special, and peculiar, *and exclusive* claim to be called *the Original States*, as well as their special and exclusive title to the protection guaranteed to them in this common heritage of property in human flesh and bones! And they were jealous, as it were, that it should be special and exclusive; and that no Colony on the continent, coming into the Union perchance after all this achievement, without having participated in the common conflict for independence, should receive the like special privilege of holding human beings in bondage, in a land so laboriously consecrated to freedom.

Hence the specialty of these guarantees and enactments. Hence, if this law of 1793 purports to have been made in pursuance of any power *vested* in Congress *by this Constitution*, it is constitutional only so far as its jurisdiction is confined to the letter and the reach of the constitutional provision. If that provision was limited to the Original States, as it certainly was, then this act cannot go beyond the limit of the original National and State domain. So far forth as it does, it becomes a mere act of Congress, based on no authority for it in the Constitution, and is therefore to that extent void in law.

But again, what was the purpose of this act?

It was, mainly, to enforce the constitutional right of reclamation, and to prescribe the mode of procedure in procuring its enforcement on behalf of the claimant. It was not necessary in doing this to go beyond the constitutional provision, or *to extend the right of reclamation* to places and circumstances of ownership or refuge not contemplated by the Constitution, and expressly stipulated against by the Ordinance of 1787. Nor do I think it was the intention of Congress to do so; else they would have made the phraseology of the act to conform to that intention. They would have said:—

"Any person held to service or labor in any of the United States, or in any of the Territories thereof,"—instead of saying: *when* a person held to labor or service (as contemplated in the Constitution) shall escape,—the person to whom such service is due may seize,—evidently looking more to the remedy of the claimant than to any extension of the right of reclamation in itself.

Hence again, I conclude that the ownership of slave property is not, and was not designed to be, recognized or protected under the Constitution, beyond the precincts of the thirteen Original States, and the Territorial domain belonging to the United States at the time of its adoption. That the constitutional provision does not recognize or protect it even in the National Territorial domain then belonging to the United States, and that it cannot be constitutionally recognized or protected even there, by any law of Congress, if the Constitution is to be regarded as having abrogated the political compact contained in the Ordinance of 1787. The only National protective recognition given to the ownership of slave property in the Territorial domain of the United States, by providing for its reclamation in said territory, was guaranteed by that Ordinance. If that compact was superseded or annulled by the later compact of the Constitution; if the two do not co-exist in such wise as to form one national compact on the subject,—then the provision as contained in the Constitution becomes the sole national compact in reference to it, and there is no power in Congress under the Constitution to extend the right of reclamation beyond that provision. Any law for the enforcement of it beyond that limit becomes unconstitutional and void.

Still it must be admitted that there were, and are, good and substantial reasons, reasons founded in equity and good conscience, why the constitutional provision should be, and has been, extended to the recognition of Slavery and to the protection of the ownership of slave property, in States formed out of the Territorial domain belonging to the United States previous to the adoption of the Constitution; or which was a part of any one of the Original States, and erected into a State after its adoption. The Constitution provides for the admission of such new States into the Union.

ARTICLE IV., SEC. 3. "New States may be admitted, by the Congress, into this Union; but no new State shall be formed or erected within the jurisdiction of any other State; nor any State formed by the junction of two or more States, without the consent of the Legislatures of the States concerned, as well as of the Congress."

But this provision clearly refers only to new States formed out of the then existing Territorial domain of the United States, or out of the then Territorial domain of some one or more of the then existing Original States, whether before or after its cession to the United States. This is evident from the fact that there was no other source from which a new State could originate. The provision could not have any wider reference. Every other political community on the continent of North America was then a Colony of some Foreign Power, owing allegiance to some Foreign Potentate, with which the United States were at peace. Treaties of amity and commerce existed between them: and to suppose that this provision of the Constitution contemplated any application of any such colony for admission into this Union as an Independent State, or that it could have any such possible reference or intention, is to suppose that the framers of it were guilty of the grossest treachery and deceit toward those powers with which they professed and avowed themselves to be at amity. Such duplicity and baseness were not a characteristic of our revolutionary fathers. They were straight-forward, out-spoken, honorable men, and had they intended any such thing they would have said:—

"Any Colony now existing on the Continent of North America, may be admitted by the Congress into this Union," etc. Such would have been their language, for such was their way of speaking out their intentions. In the Articles of Confederation they had said:—

ARTICLE XI. Canada acceding to this Confederation, *and joining in the measures of the United States*, shall be admitted into and entitled to *all the advantages* of this Union. But no other Colony shall be admitted into the same, unless such admission be agreed to by nine States.

Does not this provision demonstrate the fact as well as the reasonableness of the restriction which we put upon the admission of new States into this Union? There were privileges and benefits in the Union which were not to be gratuitously distributed or given away. There were *advantages to be purchased* only by "joining in the measures of the United States," so called, to achieve their Independence.

Hence those Colonies which had neglected to *join in those measures* were excluded, intentionally excluded from its benefits, forever thereafter, and no provision was contemplated for their after admission, by the framers of the Constitution.

Yet it was just and equitable that the people inhabiting in the then Territorial domain of the United States, whether State or National, which should thereafter seek admission into the Federal Union as one of the brotherhood of States, should receive the full benefit of the provisions in the Constitution which recognized Slavery and protected the ownership of slave property in the precincts of the Original States, of which they were originally a part. It was just and right, having *joined in the measures* of the United States during their revolutionary struggle, that they should not be deprived of any of *the advantages* accorded to the Original States under the Constitution, when any one of them came to be "received and admitted into this Union as a new and entire member of the United States of America." It was also just and right that the provisions of the political compact contained in the Ordinance of 1787, to which they also were parties, should be applied to protect them in their ownership of slave property escaped into any one of *the said* Territories of the United States.

But more than this, when the Revolutionary

Congress appealed to the Colonies to cede this Territory for the common benefit of such of them as should become members of the Federal Fraternity of States, in order to promote the ratification of the Articles of Confederation, "it pledged itself, that if the lands were ceded as recommended, they should be disposed of for the common benefit of the United States, and be settled and formed into distinct Republican States, ***which should become members*** of the Federal Union, and ***have the same rights*** of sovereignty, freedom, and independence, as the other States."* Hence originated this provision in the Constitution for the admission of New States. It was but carrying out this pledge of the Revolutionary Congress made before the establishment of the Union under the Confederation. *See Hickey's* CONSTITUTION, pp. 421, 422. Journals of Congress, 1780.

Hence it is, that we must concede the right of reclamation, and the power of Congress to enforce it, in the Original States, and in the New States formed out of the Original Territorial domain of the United States, although it is not provided for in the strict letter of the Constitution. Hence also we concede the right of representation apportioned on the slave population in such New States.

But no like reason can be given for the recognition or protection of Slavery beyond those limits.

* See Dred Scott case, p. 39.

On the contrary, everything, even to the rigid letter and the spirit of the Constitution, is against it. When the recognition given to Slavery or the protection guaranteed to the ownership of slave property reaches beyond the limits of the Territorial domain comprehended within the original precincts of the Thirteen Original States, it reaches beyond the constitutional limit; it reaches beyond all equitable and just claims to a protection derived under the Constitution, or under the Ordinance of 1787, or under the Law of 1793. It becomes an enactment for the extension of Slavery, and there is no authority for it in either.

IV.

I repeat, the Constitutional theory of the national recognition of Slavery was a theory of restriction. It had its first development in the Ordinance of 1787, prohibiting it in the Territory North-West of the river Ohio. It was further avowed in the restrictive provision of the Constitution itself, and in the act declaring the Ordinance to be in conformity with the Constitution. And whenever opportunity offered, in consistence with those peculiar relations and obligations which existed between the Original States which had "joined in the measures of the United States" during the Revolution, the National Legislature prohibited and restrained its extension except only by its natural increase. While it recognized and protected the existing ownership of slave property within the prescribed limits, provided such ownership was the fruit of any importation made previous to the year 1808, it deprecated and condemned Slavery itself. Else what means the act of March twenty-second, 1794? entitled—

AN ACT to prohibit the carrying on the Slave Trade from the United States to any Foreign place or Country. Which provides,—

"SECTION 1. *Be it enacted by the Senate and House of Representatives in Congress assembled*, That no citizen of the United States, or Foreigner, or any other person coming into or residing within the same, shall, for himself, or any other person whatsoever, either as master, factor, or owner, build, fit, equip, load, or otherwise prepare any ship or vessel, within any port or place of the said United States; nor shall cause any ship or vessel to sail from any port or place within the same, for the purpose of carrying on any trade or traffic in slaves, to any foreign country, or for the purpose of procuring from any foreign kingdom, place, or country, the inhabitants of such kingdom, place, or country, to be transferred to any foreign country, port, or place, whatsoever, to be sold or disposed of as slaves; and if any ship or vessel shall be so fitted out as aforesaid, for the said purposes, or shall be caused to sail so as aforesaid, every such ship or vessel, her tackle, furniture, apparel, and other appurtenances, shall be forfeited to the United States; and shall be liable to be seized, prosecuted, and condemned, in any of the Circuit Courts, or District Courts, for the district where the said ship or vessel may be found and seized, as aforesaid."

Was not this act a decided condemnation of Slavery and the Slave Trade? And what can be more expressive on this point than the act of May tenth, 1800? entitled AN ACT in addition to the act entitled an act to prohibit the carrying on the Slave Trade from the United States to any Foreign place or Country; and which provides,—

"SECTION 1. *Be it enacted, etc.,* That it shall be unlawful for any citizen of the United States, or other person residing within the United States, directly or indirectly to hold, or to have any right or property in any vessel employed or made use of in the transportation or carrying of slaves *from one Foreign country or place to another;* and any right or property belonging as aforesaid, shall be forfeited, and may be libelled and condemned for the use of the person who shall sue for the same; and such person transgressing the prohibition aforesaid, shall also forfeit and pay a sum of money equal to double the value of the right or property in such vessel, which he held, as aforesaid; and shall also forfeit a sum of money equal to double the value of the interest which he may have had in the slaves, which, at any time, have been transported and carried in such vessel, after the passing of this act, and against the form thereof." 2 *U. S. Stat. at large*, 70.

Was not this act aimed against the extension of Slavery? Was it not expressive of a severe determination to put an end to a traffic which was becoming a too prolific source of its increase in the United States, and against which the public sentiment of the nation was already at war? What else, again, originated the act of February twenty-eighth, 1803? entitled AN ACT to prevent the importation of certain persons into certain States, where, by the laws thereof, their admission is prohibited. Which provided that "after April first, 1803, no importation of slaves should be made into any port or place of the United States, which port or place shall be situated in any State, which has by law prohibited, or shall prohibit, such importation or admission." 2 *U. S. Stat. at large*, 205.

Why this coming up of the power of the National Sovereignty to aid and to encourage the individual state in its efforts to prevent the extension, and if possible the increase, of Slavery within its limits? What is it if not a condemnation of Slavery, and evidence of an intention to put an end to its extension beyond the natural increase in those states where it then existed, and might, perchance, thereafter continue to exist?

Why, again, was it that in May, 1800, in the "Act to divide the Territory of the United States North-West of the river Ohio into two separate districts, thereby establishing *the Indiana Territory*, a government was established over it "in all respects similar to that provided by the Ordinance of 1787," and declaring "the inhabitants to be entitled to enjoy all and singular the rights, privileges, and advantages guaranteed and secured to the people by the said Ordinance, one of which was the exclusion of Slavery?

But if anything more were wanting to settle this question, we have it still more decisively in the act of March second, 1807, entitled An Act to prohibit the importation of slaves into any port or place within the jurisdiction of the United States, from and after the first day of January one thousand eight hundred and eight, which provides,—

"SECTION I. *Be it enacted by the Senate and House of Representatives of the United States of America in Congress assembled*, That from and after the first day of January one thousand eight hundred and eight, it shall not be lawful to import, or bring into the United States, or the territory thereof, from any foreign kingdom, place, or country, any negro, mulatto, or person of color, with intent to hold, sell, or dispose of such negro, mulatto or person of color, as a slave, or to be held to service or labor." 2 *U. S. Stat. at large*, 426.

So also we have the later Act of April twentieth, 1818, made in addition to the *Act* of March second, 1807, and prohibiting the importation of colored persons as slaves, and also the Act of March third, 1819, made in addition to the Act prohibiting the Slave Trade; wherein and whereby the President of the United States is authorized and empowered "to cause any of the armed vessels of the United States to be employed to cruise on any of the coasts of the United States, or Territories thereof, or of the coasts of Africa, or elsewhere, where he may judge attempts may be made to carry on the Slave Trade, by citizens or residents of the United States, in contravention of the Acts of Congress prohibiting the same." And to invest the commanders of said cruising vessels with power to seize and take the same. 3 *U. S. Stat. at large*, 533.

So also the Act of May fifteenth, 1820, entitled "An Act to continue in force An Act to protect the commerce of the United States, and to punish the crime of Piracy;" which makes the forcibly "confining, detaining, or aiding to confine or detain any negro or mulatto person not a slave, on board of any ship or vessel with intent to make such person a slave," piracy, and punishable with death. 3 *U. S. Stat. at large*, 600.

Are not all these enactments demonstrations that in the view of the men of that day, the recognition given to Slavery and the ownership of slave property in the United States, by the National Sovereignty, was restrictive and not intended to admit its lawful existence, or to encourage, or to promotè its extension, beyond the natural increase of an already existing slave population?

V.

I have thus pointed out the nature and extent of the recognition given to Slavery in the United States by the National Sovereignty, under the Constitution. I have shown, I think conclusively, that the recognition thus given to it and the protection thus guaranteed to the ownership of slave property was originally based on the theory of its restriction, and not of its enlargement; of the suppression and not the extension of Slavery itself. That the utmost limit of its protective recognition was comprehended within the precincts of the Thirteen Original States, and the Territorial domain belonging to the United States when the Constitution was adopted. I therefore call this the first great National era of Slavery in this country. Whatever agitations it may have occasioned, whatever conflicts it may have originated during this era, either in or out of Congress, were originated within the limits specified, and determined by a reference to these admitted constitutional and equitable powers of the National Legislature over it, in the given circumstances.

I call this also the Constitutional limit to its recognition and protection by the National Sovereignty. But in this I do not mean to say, or affirm, that it may not be, or is not, otherwise recognized and protected, or that in its after extension beyond this limit it exists without any efficient or protective recognition. And this brings me to consider the true basis of its recognition beyond that derived under the Constitution. This, I maintain, originates in a source *outside of the Constitution.* In the opening of a new, a more interesting, and a more exciting era in our history on this subject of slavery. An era itself originating in a contingency not anticipated by the framers of the Constitution; not anticipated by the States, or the people of the States which ratified it; not anticipated by the first, the second, or even the third Congress; not anticipated by Washington, or by Adams, or by Jefferson; not anticipated by any of the prominent and far-seeing statesmen of that early day, and consequently not provided for in the Constitution. That contingency was, the extension of the National domain and Sovereignty of the United States beyond the constitutional limit, by the acquisition of Foreign Territory.

The purchase of "the Domain and Sovereignty of the Louisiana Territory, its dependencies, and the

Islands adjacent," from France in 1803, was an addition to the domain and jurisdiction of the United States not anticipated by its framers, and not provided for by the Constitution. It has already been observed that the Articles of Confederation provided for the admission of Canada and other Colonies on the American Continent, into the Confederacy. But no such or similar provision is found in the Constitution. The omission was not unintentional. It was undoubtedly designed to restrict the Union *under this Constitution* to the Colonies which had originally and all along acceded to the League of Union under the Martial Manifesto, and under the Declaration of Independence, and to the Federal Alliance under the Confederation; and had *joined in the measures of the United States* in achieving their Independence. To these, called in the favorite and exclusive phraseology of the framers of the Constitution the Original States, were reserved all the advantages of the Confederated Union; and all the peculiar privileges, guarantees and stipulations contained in the political Compact of the Ordinance of 1787, and in the Compact of the Constitution, on the subject of Slavery; which, *in the same sense and to the same extent*, could not be conceded to any other. Theirs was the privilege of transporting their slave property "from any port or place in one State to any port or place in another State." Theirs was the privilege of a representation in Congress apportioned on a slave population. Theirs the privilege of reclaiming their slave property escaping into any other State, or Territory, of the United States. And these advantages were exclusively guaranteed to them under the Constitution, and there is no provision in it for their further extension.

True, the Constitution provided for the admission of New States into the Union, but this, as I have shown, and shall hereafter demonstrate, was a provision peculiarly pointing to the original National and State domain, and limited precisely to Territory within the then precincts of the National Sovereignty.

True, Congress had power, under the Constitution, "to make all needful rules and regulations respecting the Territory, or other property, belonging to the United States." But this again, was within the limits specified, for it certainly could not refer to Territory not then belonging to the United States.

The purchase of foreign Territory was a new compact of the National Sovereignty, made independently of any provision in the Constitution, and not a purchase under or by virtue of any warrant for it in the Constitution. Nor can it be claimed that the constitutional provision was intended to recognize Slavery or protect the ownership of slave-property, anywhere and everywhere. Congress could not thus make itself a partner in, or the protector of, a traffic which the

5*

framers of the Constitution had condemned and prohibited by the severest penalties, by simply buying up an entire new Sovereignty overrun with Slaves and Slavery; and that too a Sovereignty from which they had already interdicted the importation of slaves into the United States.

The Compact of the Constitution was, in every sense, and in all senses of it, a compact for freedom and not for Slavery. It did not in any sense recognize Slavery itself. It only recognized *the right of service derived under an existing ownership* of slave property. And while it guaranteed its protection to those who, with the inherited weight of a slave property on their shoulders, had "borne the heat and burden of the day" of the Revolution, it did not intend to recognize the same claim to its protection in other and alien Colonies which had stood aloof from the struggle, even if perchance they might thereafter come within the pale of its political association and sovereign jurisdiction. I say it did not intend it, because *first*, no such accession to the Union could thereafter be made under circumstances entitling the new member to claim it; and *second*, because no such accession was then either anticipated or desired.

This protective recognition of the ownership of Slave property, I repeat, was an exception from the great rule of freedom, made in favor of the Original States, because they had "joined in the measures of the United States" in achieving their National Sovereignty. Canada had not joined in those measures; other Colonies had not joined in those measures, and therefore all were excluded from the common benefits of the achievement; and none but the Original States, or States formed out of them, were suffered to participate in the peculiar privileges given to the ownership of Slave-property within the limits, for these very peculiar reasons.

Call Slavery a curse if you will, still they must take the curse if they would have the blessing of Independence. They could not throw it back upon the Parent State, whose Sovereignty over them they had now repudiated. The inheritance was theirs, they had assumed the burden of it, and they must make the best of the incumbrance; the best for themselves, the best for freedom, the best for humanity. They did so; and thus it stood so far as the Constitutional recognition of it was concerned until the subsequent acquisition of *the Louisiana Territory* gave rise to the question as to the power of Congress to extend Slavery under the Constitution. The purchase, in itself, was nothing more or less than a compact between the United States as a Sovereignty, and France as another Sovereignty, for the conveyance of the said Territory to the former. And it was, as I have said, a compact outside and independent of the Constitution. So far as the mere acquisition of Territory was concerned, it presented no difficulty. When the bargain was concluded and the transfer of title was actually made, it came under the jurisdiction of the National Sovereignty of the United States, subject to its government and control. It brought with it, however, a subject the very existence of which was in conflict with the Spirit of the Constitution, and the existing laws of the United States, made in pursuance of it: and that was Slavery; which involved the recognition of it beyond the constitutional limit, and within the prohibitions of the Laws of the United States.

On the thirty-first day of October, 1803, an act was passed by Congress to enable the President of the United States to take possession of the Territory ceded by France to the United States by the treaty concluded at Paris on the thirtieth of April last; and for the Temporary Government thereof." 2. *U. S. Stat. at Large*, p. 245.

On the twenty-sixth day of March, 1804, an act was passed, "Erecting Louisiana into two Territories, and providing for the temporary government thereof." *Ibid.*, 283.

This act designated the lands lying South of the Mississippi Territory as *the Territory of Orleans;* while the other portion was designated *the District of Louisiana*, and the government of it was placed under the Governor and Judges of the Indiana Territory, one of the Districts into which the Territory North-West of the River Ohio had been distributed. This act also prohibited the importation or bringing of Slaves into the said Territory *from any port or place without* the United States. It also prohibited the importation or transportation of Slaves into the said Territory, *from any port or place in* the United States, which were brought into the United States after May first, 1789. And further provided, that no Slave " should be, directly or indirectly, introduced into said Territory except by a Citizen of the United States, removing therein for actual settlement, and being, at the time, a *bona-fide* owner of such Slave or Slaves." In case any Slave or Slaves were brought into the said Territory, in violation of these provisions, or either of them, it was provided, that such Slave or Slaves should "*thereupon be entitled to and receive his or her freedom.*"

Thus, on the very threshold of taking possession of this newly acquired Territory, Congress emphatically declares that it was not the intention of the National Sovereignty to promote the extension of Slavery. On the contrary, it announces the sentiment of the Government and the people of the United States to be against its extension. Slavery, however, had already obtained in some portions of this vast domain, and the people inhabiting therein claimed protection in the ownership of their Slave-property under the third Article of the Convention with France, which provided,

"The inhabitants of the ceded Territory shall be incorporated into the Union of the United States, and admitted as soon as possible according to the principles of the Federal Constitution, to the enjoyment of all the rights, advantages, and immunities *of citizens* of the United States; *and in the mean time* they *shall be protected* in the free enjoyment of their liberty, *property*, and the religion which they profess."

As this provision in the Convention, or Treaty, was made the basis of opposition to the restrictions imposed upon Slavery in this Territory, it may be well, in passing, to note its phraseology. It was claimed that the stipulation guaranteed the recognition and protection of Slavery. The words are, "*the inhabitants* of the ceded Territory shall be protected," etc. Now who were the inhabitants? Not the free *citizens* or *free* inhabitants, or the *white* inhabitants, but *the inhabitants*, without any distinction as to color, caste, or condition, shall be thus incorporated into the Union, and admitted to the enjoyment of all the rights, advantages, and immunities *of citizens of the United States.* In the mean time, that is, before they become thus incorporated, and until they are thus incorporated, they, that is, *the inhabitants of the ceded Territory*, "shall be protected" both by the United States and France,—"in the free enjoyment of their *liberty*, *property*, and the religion they profess."

So far from guaranteeing protection to Slavery, the stipulation does not even recognize its distinct-tive existence: and if *the inhabitants* of the Territory, without exception or qualification, were to be protected in the *free* enjoyment of their liberty, why not the slaves?

But conceding that the stipulation was intended to protect the ownership of slave property in the said Territory, and that it bound the United States to recognize and protect it there, it evidently did not do so by virtue of any provision in the Constitution, or beyond the time when the said Territory should be incorporated into the Union. Nor did the idea of its incorporation into the Union, refer to its being erected into a State and becoming in this wise a member of the Federal body politic. It was incorporated into the Union for all the purposes specified, and its inhabitants were admitted "as soon as possible according to the *principles* of the Federal Constitution, to the enjoyment of all the rights, advantages, and immunities *of citizens* of the United States," the moment the United States took possession, assumed jurisdiction, and established a government over it. There could be no just claim or pretence that the said Territory, or any portion of it, should be admitted into the Union as a State, *per force* of the stipulation contained in the Convention with France. As soon as it was incorporated into and became a part of the Territorial domain of the United States, the stipulation with France was fully performed, and at an end. It became thenceforth subject exclusively to the Sovereignty of the United States.

Nor could it, or any portion of it, be admitted into the Union as a State, *per force* of any provision in the Constitution. Because, as I have shown, there was no provision in the Constitution which contemplated the purchase of Foreign Territory, or the creation of New States out of Foreign Territory.

Nor, hence, could Slavery be recognized and protected there *per force* of any provision in the Constitution. Because, again, there was no protection guaranteed to Slavery by the Constitution beyond its own original jurisdiction, or the obligation to protect it in the Original States and Territory. But I do not say, or mean to intimate, that the States and people then composing the National Sovereignty called the United States, could not make a compact for the recognition of Slavery and the protection of the ownership of Slave property in the newly acquired Territory, *independently of the Constitution.* And here is the very gist of the controversy, the very oversight of our day. An existing mercantile firm may stipulate with a clerk of the concern to admit him into the copartnership as a new and entire member thereof, on terms and conditions entirely distinct from, and independent of, the original articles between themselves; at the same time extending to him, or reserving to themselves exclusively, any peculiar advantages of those original articles. So here; it is a new compact between the National Sovereignty and the people of the newly acquired Territory, for their admission into the Union as an independent State. As inhabitants of its Territorial domain they are subjects of the National Sovereignty; and are in no sense sovereign, or independent of it, except so far as the Congressional Act establishing the Territorial government may vest them with a portion of its sovereignty. And while it may convey to them so much of its sovereignty as is necessary to build up and sustain their local government and institutions, and may guarantee to them protection in the ownership of their Slave-property, such compact cannot base itself upon any provision in the Constitution, nor do they thereby become independent of its supremacy. Whether made in the organization of a Territorial Government, or by an Act of admission into the Union as a State, it is a compact independent of the Constitution. The new Sovereignty is acting in its Sovereign capacity and

6

not under the Constitution. But of this more particularly hereafter.

VI.

On the third day of March, 1805, Congress passed an Act entitled "An Act further to provide for the government of *The District of Louisiana*," declaring that "all that part of the country ceded by France to the United States under the general name of *Louisiana*, which by the Act of 1804 was erected into a separate District, to be called *The District of Louisiana*, shall henceforth be known and designated by the name and title of *The Territory of Louisiana*, the government whereof is organized as follows," &c.

On the twentieth of February, 1811, an Act was passed—"*To enable* the people of *the Territory of Orleans* to form a Constitution and State government, and for the admission of such State into the Union on an equal footing with the Original States, and for other purposes"—2 *U. S. Stat. at Large*, *p.* 648, which was followed on the eighth of April, 1812, by an Act entitled "An Act for the admission of the State of Louisiana (the Territory of Orleans) into the Union, and to extend the Laws of the United States to said State.

On the fourth of June, 1812, an Act was passed entitled "An Act providing for the government of

The Territory of Missouri," which enacted that "The Territory heretofore called *Louisiana* shall hereafter be called *Missouri,*"—over which a temporary government was established by the same Act.

Mississippi was admitted into the Union as a Slave State, on the tenth day of December, 1817, her constitution being declared by Congress to be "Republican, and in conformity with the principles of the Articles of Compact between the Original States and the people and States of the Territory North-West of the River Ohio." Thus recognizing the existing integrity of the Ordinance of 1787.

The phraseology of the resolution of admission declared—"that the State of Mississippi shall be one, and is hereby declared to be one of the United States of America, and admitted into the Union on an equal footing with the Original States, in all respects whatever."

The Eastern part of this Territory had previously been erected into a separate Territory under the name of Alabama, by Act of Congress, March third, 1817. The whole of the Mississippi Territory was a part of the Original States of South Carolina and Georgia, and was by them ceded to the United States for the common benefit. Alabama was admitted into the Union, December fourteenth, 1819.

The States erected out of the North-West Territory were, Ohio, admitted April 30th, 1802; Indiana, Dec. 11th, 1816; Illinois, Dec. 3d, 1818.

The question of Slavery was not materially discussed upon the admission of any of those States into the Union, which were formed out of Territory comprehended within the precincts of the United States at the adoption of the Constitution. Still, it must be observed, that in the Compact for their admission, the integrity of the Articles contained in the Ordinance of 1787 was stipulated as a condition precedent to their admission.

Louisiana was the first State formed out of the Territory ceded by France to the United States. The existence of Slavery within her limits was so general that her admission into the Union as a Slave State did not give rise to any particular controversy with reference to it; And it must be admitted that with even this addition to its numerical strength in the United States, a great deal had been accomplished in the way of suppressing Slavery generally, by the purchase of this Territory. It was thus brought under the Act prohibiting the Slave Trade, as well as other restrictive laws of the United States in reference to it. In this view alone, the evil of its extension if it can properly be called an extension of it, was more than counterbalanced by the prohibitions and restraints to which it became subject under the jurisdiction of the United States. The exaction that her laws, judicial proceedings, and records, should be in the same language used in the United States, might well be regarded as a sufficient equivalent for the recognition given to Slavery, and the protection guaranteed to the ownership of her Slave property, under the Laws of the United States. All this, however, be it remembered, was the subject of a new compact between the proposed State of Louisiana and the National Sovereignty. It could not be claimed or conceded under the Constitution.

CHAPTER II.

SLAVERY OUTSIDE OF THE CONSTITUTION.

I.

THE Confederation was a compact between the Colonies as States claiming an independence of each other as well as of Great Britain. The Constitution was a compact between the people of the United States claiming in themselves a Sovereignty independent both of the State and Federal Supremacy. Hence the great defect of the Confederation was, that the Sovereignty wrested from Great Britain was given to the States in severalty, while no provision was made for a National Government of supreme authority and general jurisdiction. The Constitution was designed to remedy this defect, and was based on the theory of an existing National Sovereignty in the people of the Thirteen Original States, acquired by conquest from Great Britain, and limited in its jurisdiction and supremacy only by the precincts described in the Definitive Treaty executed between the Commissioners of the two nations at Paris, September third, 1783.

The *Constitutional* National Sovereignty of The United States, therefore, was in the Confederacy composed of the people of those Original States alone. Upon every admission of a new State into this Union, from that day to the present, this distinctive Sovereignty has not only been distinctly recognized, but also emphatically declared, in the compact of admission "on an equal footing with the Original States."

If then, the admission of Ohio, Indiana, Illinois, Mississippi, Alabama, Tennessee, and Kentucky, did not create a National Sovereignty different from that recognized and provided for by the Constitution, the same cannot be said of the admission of Louisiana. Not only was this state the offspring of a jurisdiction extended beyond the Constitutional limit, but its admission into the Union "on an equal footing with the Original States," was an addition to the National Confederacy, which made its government a new and a different National Sovereignty from that contemplated by the Constitution. Hence, all its acts done in its Sovereign capacity, must be considered as done independently of any original Constitutional authority, whether made, or purporting to be made, in conformity with the general principles of the Constitution or not.

This peculiarity in the formation and character of our National Government, is especially important to be observed in considering this question of Slavery, in connection with the admission of new States into the Union, if we would arrive at a correct comprehension of the theory of its National recognition and relations. I have shown this theory under the Constitution to have been one of restriction and not of expansion, and that it was limited, in its practical application, to the Original precincts of the United States as established under the Definitive Treaty with Great Britain. The acquisition of the Louisiana Territory was the introduction of a new Slave-population within the embrace of our National Sovereignty, the existence and ownership of which claimed anew its National recognition and protection. This was guaranteed to the existing servitude in the State of Louisiana by the compact for her admission into the Union. But that, strictly speaking, could not be called an extension of Slavery itself, inasmuch as it already had an existence there before the cession of the Territory to the United States by France. The real material question of its extension originated with the application of the people inhabiting in the Territory called the Territory of Missouri, to be admitted into the Union as a State. The origin and history of this application, therefore, is both interesting and important in this connection.

But before entering upon it I would premise—that every new member admitted into union with the Original States, out of Territory foreign to the original domain of those States and of the United States, must necessarily be subject to a new and distinct political compact for its admission, made between it and the said Original States; or, between it and the States composing the National Sovereignty at the time of its admission. It could not derive any claim to admission by virtue of any provision in the Constitution, for neither it, or the now existing Confederacy, was known to the Constitution. In this respect evidently it differed in position from a State formed out of Territory within the original, recognized, Constitutional domain; and for whose admission provision was expressly made in the Constitution. Hence the right of the New Confederacy to dictate terms and impose conditions in the former case, beyond the strict letter of the Constitution, which it could not with the same justice or propriety exact or enforce in the latter case.

And again, the purchase of "the domain and Sovereignty of the Louisiana Territory, its dependencies, and the Islands adjacent," from France, in 1803, being an addition to the domain and jurisdiction of the United States not anticipated and not provided for by its framers, necessarily falls under some other source of jurisdiction than that derived under the Constitution. It not only enlarged the Territorial precincts of the New Sovereignty, called the United States, beyond the Constitutional limits, but it also derived to this New Sovereignty a dominion over the new Territory and the people inhabiting therein, which the people themselves had no share in creating. The purchase, as I have said, was a new compact, made with France by the then existing National Sovereignty of the United States independently of the Constitution. It was a compact by the United States as a Sovereignty, with France as another Sovereignty, for the purchase by the former of "the domain and Sovereignty" of the latter, over Territory with which neither the Constitution, nor the States, nor the people of the United States, nor the people inhabiting in the said Territory, had anything to do. The New Sovereignty purchased, be it remembered, not only the domain but also *the Imperial Sovereignty* of France over it, and thereby as an inevitable consequence, acquired the *Imperial right to govern it.* This right was sovereign and exclusive, so far as the people then inhabiting, or thereafter to inhabit, in the said Territory were concerned. Now the question is, who is sovereign over this same Territory? The people inhabiting therein, or the Sovereignty which purchased it? Again, the question is, who shall say upon what terms, or subject to what conditions, the people inhabiting in the said Territory may be erected into an independent State, and admitted as such into Union with the States composing the National Confederacy, with the same rights of Sovereignty, freedom, and Independence? Who does not see that herein is involved a relinquishment on the part of the National Government of the imperial supremacy which it purchased from France, at a cost of six million francs? Who does not see that the transfer from such a Territorial to a State Organization, involves a declaration of independence on the part of the people inhabiting in the Territory, or a relinquishment of its supremacy over them on the part of the National Sovereignty of the United States? The very idea supposes a condition of political elevation which cannot be created without depriving the National Sovereignty of a part at least of its own supremacy. Not only so, but it also places the New Organization in the relations and position of a copartner in the

Sovereignty residing in the National Confederacy. And has the National Sovereignty no voice in this political transformation? May it not say whether at all, or upon what terms, or subject to what fundamental conditions, it will consent to this new creation? Consent to relinquish its own supremacy in its own Territory, and to admit the new State, thus created, into the great Federal Copartnership? Certainly it must. In the case of Louisiana, as we have seen, it exercised this right by the fundamental condition that her administration and laws, her judicial proceedings and records, should be in the English language.

This, I repeat, was a compact made outside of the Constitution. Yet it was an exercise of the Sovereign capacity of the New Sovereignty, forming a political compact in reference to a Territory and to matters entirely within its jurisdiction independently of the Constitution: and so of the Missouri Territory. The transfer of a community so situated from a dependent Territorial to an independent State Organization, is a change of political condition and relations in itself of vast importance not only to the people inhabiting in the new Territory, but also to the people and States composing the National Sovereignty called the United States. It is a transition which makes it an entirely different political organization, sustaining new and peculiar relations of freedom, sovereignty, and independence, to and in the great Confederated Republic. To the latter, therefore, as well as to the former, it becomes a question of peculiar interest—upon what terms and subject to what conditions shall we consent to this new political organization, and admit it to this position of independence and associated Sovereignty ?

It cannot, then, be rightfully claimed that the National Sovereignty shall have no voice in fixing the terms of this change of condition and admission into the Union. Especially is this so where the National Government is called upon to recognize the existence or extension of Slavery beyond the restrictive provisions of its own Constitution and Laws.

And just such was the application made by the people of the Territory of Missouri. It was, I repeat, for leave to transform themselves from a Territorial to a State Organization, and as such State Organization to have their independence of the National Sovereignty so far conceded as to permit them to establish a State Constitution and Government, that they might be admitted into the Union as an individual State, with the same rights of sovereignty, freedom, and independence as were inherent in the Original States. The very application involved the admission of their dependence upon the National Sovereignty, and that its consent was necessary to enable them to form such a State Organization, which involved also the admission that the same Sovereignty had the power and the right to prescribe the terms and conditions upon which this new organization might be made.

But the petition of the people of Missouri was not merely for leave to erect themselves into a State Organization, it was also for admission into the Union under such State Constitution, " on an equal footing with the Original States in all respects whatever." Nor was this all; and here originated the difficulty. Slavery had extended itself, and was now existing in the Territory proposed to be erected into an independent State and thus admitted into the Union. The proposition therefore was to admit Missouri as a Slave State, which involved three very essential and important features; these were—

I. The recognition of Slavery therein as a State institution, by the National Sovereignty.

II. The guarantee of protection to the ownership of her Slave property by the Laws of the United States, as in the Original States under the Constitution.

III. That the right of representation in the National legislature should be apportioned on her Slave population, as in the Original States.

This, it will be observed, was a recognition of Slavery in which not only the people, but also all the States of the whole Union, were alike deeply interested. These were the prominent and vital principles embraced in the application for the admission of Missouri, the results of which were to inaugurate and establish, for all time, the policy of the New Sovereignty in reference to this subject of Slavery in its newly acquired domain.

On the eighteenth day of December 1818, the Speaker of the House of Representatives of the United States, presented before that body, a memorial of the Legislative Council and House of Representatives of the Territory of Missouri, in the name and on behalf of the people of the said Territory, praying that they be permitted to form a Constitution and State Government, with the boundaries thereof as described in said petition, and admitted into the Union on an equal footing with the Original States. This petition was received, read, and appropriately referred. Upon which reference a Bill was subsequently reported by the Committee, "*To enable* the people of the Territory of Missouri to form a State Government," etc., and was made the order of the day for February thirteenth, 1819.

The introduction of this Bill, I repeat, involved the recognition and extension of Slavery to an extent not before anticipated. It became at once a question of national and absorbing interest to the people and the States of the whole Union. It brought more directly before them than ever before, the issue of its restriction or extension. It had extended and with an almost imperceptible progress was now stealing its way over that immense Territory, and the appalling questions were, How far shall it go? Where shall its progress end? All the Original States were alike parties to the purchase of the Territory, and all were alike interested and startled by the issue. They had cut off the foreign source of its increase, by abolishing and prohibiting the Slave-Trade. They had restricted it within their own limits at home; and they thought they had guarded against its further extension, when lo! it rises before their astonished vision, knocking at the doors of Congress, claiming to be further extended, recognized, and protected, by the National Sovereignty. True, they had already recognized it beyond the original limit by the purchase from France. They had already adopted and agreed to protect it beyond that limit by the admission of Louisiana, and now the question is forced upon them,—Shall it go any further? Shall it be still extended, and recognized, and protected, by the National Sovereignty?

Hence it was that the introduction of the Bill for the admission of Missouri into the Union, became one of intense national interest and importance. It developed the necessity of some definite national policy on the subject of Slavery. It presented new and very grave questions, involving principles, interests, and sequences, as momentous and extensive as any that had ever agitated the nation. Those who were instrumental in framing the Constitution, as I have said, had not provided for any such emergency. They had not anticipated it. Nor had they anticipated, expected, or even desired, that Slavery should be a permanent institution in this Confederacy under the sanction of the National Government.

On the thirteenth day of February 1819, the Bill for the admission of Missouri being the order of the day, in the House of Representatives, Mr. Tallmadge of New York, proposed to amend by adding to it the following clause:

" *And provided*, that the further introduction of Slavery, or involuntary servitude, be prohibited, except for the punishment of crimes whereof the party shall have been duly convicted: And that all children born within the said State after the admission thereof into the Union, shall be free at the age of twenty-five years."

The justice and general propriety of this amendment was so apparent, that it was adopted by the House, and the Bill was thereupon ordered to a third reading, was engrossed, and finally passed on the seventeenth of the same month. It then passed into the Senate, where it received sundry amendments, the most material of which was an amendment striking out the restriction upon Slavery. It was returned to the House with the amendments made by the Senate, all of which were concurred in except that which struck out the prohibitory clause concerning Slavery. On the question of concurring with the Senate in this amendment, the House refused to concur, and the Bill was returned to the Senate. A message was subsequently received from the Senate that they adhered to their amendment, and the Bill was lost.

Contemporaneously with this movement, on the fifteenth of December 1818, Mr. Robertson, of Kentucky, offered to the consideration of the House of Representatives a resolution in these words, viz.—

Resolved, That a Committee be appointed to enquire into the expediency of establishing a separate Territorial Government in that part of the Territory of Missouri lying south of thirty-six degrees and thirty minutes, North Latitude, which is called the Arkansas Country, which is not included in the proposed boundary of the projected State of Missouri by the Bill now before the House for the purpose of establishing a State government in part of the Territory of Missouri; and that the said Committee have leave to report by Bill or otherwise."

This resolution was adopted without opposition. On the twenty-first day of the same month, Mr. Robertson, from the Committee, reported a Bill establishing a separate Territorial government over the

7*

said Southern part of Missouri, which was read twice and committed. On the thirtieth day of January following, Mr. Scott, from the Territory of Missouri, presented to the House a petition of sundry inhabitants of the Arkansas Country, praying that a separate Territorial Government might be established for the said Country, and that Commissioners might be appointed to fix a site for the seat thereof; which was referred.

A Bill was subsequently reported on this petition, and made the order of the day for February seventeenth, when the House resolved itself into a Committee of the whole on the Bill to provide a Territorial Government for the Southern part of the Missouri Territory, called the Arkansas Country.

Mr. Taylor, of New York, moved to amend this Bill, by inserting a clause precisely similar to the amendment of Mr. Tallmadge to the Bill for the admission of Missouri, prohibiting Slavery in the new Territory. The motion was warmly and widely debated, and the range of the debate did not differ essentially from that on the Missouri Bill; except inasmuch as the issue here presented had reference to a Territorial Government, instead of the restriction being incorporated into a State Constitution, as in the case of Missouri.

Mr. Taylor's motion was, to amend the proposed

Senatorial Bill by inserting in it the following proviso, viz.—

"That the *further* introduction of Slavery, or involuntary servitude, be prohibited, except for the punishment of crimes whereof the party shall have been duly convicted: and that all children, born within the said Territory after the admission thereof into the Union, shall be free at the age of twenty-five years."

The question on this amendment was divided, and was first taken on agreeing to the first clause thereof, prohibiting the further introduction of Slavery into the Territory; which was lost. The vote was then taken on the latter part of the proposed amendment, in these words:—

"And all children born of slaves within the said Territory, shall be free, but may be held to service until the age of twenty-five years;" which was carried in the affirmative. The Bill, with the Amendment, was then ordered to be engrossed for a third reading.

II.

The Bill was again taken up on the nineteenth day of February, when Mr. Robertson, of Kentucky, moved to recommit it to a Select Committee, with instructions to strike out the amendment of Mr. Taylor, adopted by the House on the seventeenth. On taking the question on this motion the vote stood eighty-eight to eighty-eight, and was decided in the affirmative by the casting vote of the Speaker, Henry Clay. Whereupon the Bill was recommitted, and Mr. Robertson, from the Select Committee, to whom it was referred, immediately reported the Bill amended by striking out the words "And all Children born of Slaves within the said Territory shall be free, but may be held to service until the age of twenty-five years." The question on the concurrence of the House in the Report of the Select Committee, in striking out this clause, was passed in the affirmative, yeas, 89; nays, 87.

Mr. Taylor now moved to amend the Bill, by providing—" that during the existence of the Territorial Government of Arkansas, no Slaves shall be brought into the said Territory to remain therein for a longer time than nine months from the date of their arrival." After some debate thereon, Mr. Taylor modified this amendment so as to read—" that neither Slavery, or involuntary servitude, shall hereafter be introduced into said Territory, otherwise than for the punishment of crimes whereof the party shall have been duly convicted."

To this Mr. Mercer, of Virginia, proposed an amendment, by adding thereto—" *provided*, that nothing herein shall divest the inhabitants of Arkansas of the rights of property in the Slaves which they now hold, or the natural increase thereof; nor entitle to his freedom any slave carried therein and held there for a period not exceeding nine months." This proposition was rejected without a division, and the question was then taken on the amendment of Mr. Taylor, and resulted, ayes, 86; nays, 91.

Mr. Taylor now again rose, and stated, that he thought it important that some line should be designated beyond which Slavery should not be permitted, and moved, *by way of compromise*, and as an additional section to the Bill, the following:—"That neither Slavery, nor involuntary servitude, *shall hereafter be introduced* into any part of the Territory of the United States lying north of thirty-six degrees and thirty minutes, North Latitude."

Mr. Harrison, of Ohio, assented to the expediency of establishing some such line, as proposed by Mr. Taylor, but proposed, by way of amendment to Mr. T's proposition, viz.—

"That all that part of the present Territory of *Missouri*, lying north of a line to be run due west from the mouth of the River Des Moines to the Territorial boundary of the United States, shall form a part of the Territory of Michigan; and the laws now in force in the said Territory, as well as the Ordinance of Congress prohibiting Slavery, or involuntary servitude, in said Territory of Michigan, shall be in force in that part of the Missouri Territory lying North of the said East and West line."

After considerable discussion pro. and con, on these propositions, Mr. Taylor remarked, that he was satisfied from the course of the debate, as well as from conversation with members, that it was not probable that any line could be agreed upon by the House, or any compromise of opinion effected, and he therefore withdrew his proposed amendment to the Bill. Whereupon the bill was ordered to be engrossed and read a third time. On the twentieth of February it was read a third time and passed.

The Bill came up in the Senate, together with the Bill to authorize the people of Missouri to form a Constitution and State Government, on the twenty-seventh day of the same month; when, as we have before seen, the restrictive clause in the latter Bill was stricken out; and the Senate adjourned without acting finally on either Bill.

On the first day of March ensuing, the consideration of the Arkansas Territorial Bill was resumed in the Senate, and on motion of Mr. Burrill, of Rhode Island, "That the said Bill be recommitted to the Committee to whom the same was first referred, with instructions so to amend the same, that *the further introduction of Slavery*, or involuntary servitude, *within said Territory*, except for the punishment of crimes, be prohibited,"—it was determined in the negative, ayes, 14; nays, 19. The question was then taken upon the final passage of the Bill, and was decided in the affirmative.

Thus the Bill was passed by both Houses of Congress, establishing a Territorial Government over the Arkansas Country, without any provision for the restriction of Slavery therein. It must be observed, however, that while no provision was made for its prohibition, neither was any made for its protective recognition by the National Sovereignty.

The most important feature disclosed in this controversy was the element of opposition to the further extension of Slavery, either by its natural increase, or by the transfer of Slave property from States where it already existed, into the new Territory. The Slave Trade was abolished by the unanimous consent of the States and the people of the United States, and its further increase from that source was regarded as virtually at an end. The question of its extension was thus necessarily limited to these remaining sources of supply. Hence the question of its further recognition by the National Sovereignty, by permitting its transfer into this new Territory, and protecting its ownership there by the laws of the United States, was the great question which agitated the Congress and the Nation at this time.

The Bill for the Territorial Government of that

portion of the Missouri Territory, called the Arkansas Country, having been thus disposed of, the discussion and the controversy were resumed with increased excitement and interest, at the first session of the Sixteenth Congress, on the Bill for the admission of Missouri into the Union, on an equal footing with the Original States, thereby extending the recognition and protection of the National Sovereignty over Slavery within her precincts. The contest was a very excited and a very fearful one, and shook the whole union to its very foundation. It continued in its various phases to agitate both the Congress and the people of the United States from this date, down to the sixth day of March 1820, when, having passed both Houses of Congress in its present shape, it was approved by the President, and became a political Compact between the National Sovereignty of the United States and the people and States of the Union, and the people thereafter to inhabit in the said Territory, on the subject of Slavery. But to recur to its more particular history.—

On the eighth day of December, 1819, on motion of Mr. Scott, of Missouri, the several Memorials of the Legislature of the Territory of Missouri, and of the inhabitants of the said Territory, presented to the House of Representatives at the last session, relative to the erection of that Territory into a State, and its admission as such into the Union, was referred to a Select Committee. That Committee consisted of Messrs. Scott; George Robertson, of Kentucky; William Terell and George F. Strother, of Virginia; and Mr. Dewitt, of New York.

On the ninth of the same month, Mr. Scott, from this Committee, reported—"A Bill to authorize the People of the Territory of Missouri to form a State Government, and for the admission of such State into the Union on an equal footing with the Original States." The Bill was thereupon read twice, and committed to the House in Committee of the whole. It was afterward made the order of the day for the tenth day of January, 1820; when its consideration was further postponed, and made the order of the day for January twenty-fourth, ensuing; at which time Mr. Taylor, of New York, moved that its consideration be postponed to that day week, with the view of waiting the decision of the Senate on the Bill then before that body, on the same subject. This motion was lost, ayes, 87; noes, 88.

On the eighth day of December previous, the same day in which Mr. Scott moved for a Select Committee in the House, Mr. Mellen, in the Senate, presented the memorial of a Convention held in the District of Maine, praying to be admitted into the Union, as a separate and independent State, on the footing of an Original State; together with a Constitution formed in said Convention for the State of Maine; which were severally read and referred.

On the twenty-second day of the same month, Mr. Williams, of Mississippi, from the Committee to which these matters were referred, reported a Bill to the Senate, declaring the consent of Congress to the admission of Maine into the Union as a State; and the Bill passed to a second reading. On the twenty-third of December it was read a second time, and considered as in Committee of the whole. It was then amended, and the further consideration of it postponed until Tuesday, December twenty-eighth, when it was again postponed to Monday, January third, 1820.

On the twenty-ninth day of December previous, Mr. Smith laid before the Senate the Memorial of the Legislative Council and House of Representatives of the Missouri Territory, praying to be admitted into the Union, as a separate and Independent State; when the memorial was read and referred to the Judiciary Committee. On Monday, the third day of January, a message was received from the House of Representatives, informing the Senate, that the House had passed a Bill entitled—"An Act for the admission of the State of Missouri into the Union," and requesting the concurrence of the Senate therein.

Mr. Barbour, of Virginia, observed that this Bill

involved considerations of great moment; that it embraced provisions on which there were conflicting opinions, though no objection whatever was entertained to the main object of it, of which he was warmly in favor. He concluded his remarks by moving that the further consideration of it be postponed to Wednesday, January fifth, when, he said, if his present motion succeeded, he should move—

"That the Bill entitled 'A Bill declaring the consent of Congress to the admission of the State of Maine into the Union, be committed to the Committee on the Judiciary, with instructions so to amend it as to authorisé the People of Missouri to establish a State Government, and to admit such State into the Union upon an equal footing with the original States in all respects whatever.'"

The motion to postpone was opposed at considerable length, by Messrs. Mellen, Otis, and Burril, successively, on the ground of the impropriety of the delay, and also as taken in connection with the motion of which notice was given by Mr. Barbour. They argued the inexpediency of coupling the two subjects together in one Bill; and that, incidentally, the question connected with certain restrictions in the Missouri Bill on the subject of Slavery, must enter into the debate. Mr. Barbour replied; but the motion now before the Senate being simply on postponing the consideration of the Maine Bill, it was generally agreed to.

On the fifth of January, the Bill declaring the assent of the Senate to the admission of Maine into the Union, was again taken up on motion of Mr. Mellen, and the consideration thereof was postponed for four weeks.

The object of this postponement was understood to be the relinquishment of this Bill, in order to take up the Bill on the same subject, which had already passed the House of Representatives, and been received and referred to a Committee in the Senate. 35, *Annals of Congress*, 69.

On the sixth of January, Mr. Smith, from the Committee to whom the Bill for the admission of Maine had been referred, reported the same with an amendment, which amendment was—the addition thereto of the whole of the House Bill authorizing the people of Missouri to form a State Constitution, without the restrictive provision on the subject of Slavery.

Mr. Pinckney, of South Carolina, after alluding to the magnitude of the question involved in this amendment, and the importance of a full examination, clear understanding, and correct decision of it; *moved* that the consideration thereof be postponed to, and made the order of the day for Thursday next, January thirteenth, which was carried. *Ibid.* 74.

On Thursday, the thirteenth, the Senate took up the Bill from the House, for the admission of the State of Maine into the Union, together with the amendment reported thereto, by the Judiciary Committee, for the admission of Missouri; when Mr. Roberts, of Pennsylvania, rose and said, he felt it to be his duty to try the merits of these two questions, by a preliminary motion, which he offered, viz.,—"That the Bill for the admission of the State of Maine into the Union, and the amendments thereto reported, be recommitted to the Judiciary Committee, with instructions so to modify its provisions as to admit the State of Maine into the Union, divested of the amendment embracing Missouri."

The proposition contained in the Report of the Committee, by way of amendment to the Bill for the admission of Maine, admitting Missouri without any restriction upon the subject of Slavery, is evidence of the high degree of excitement to which this question had given rise. That Maine was entitled to admission into the Union under the provisions of the Constitution, there could be no doubt. And she might well ask to be admitted "on an equal footing with the Original States, in all respects whatever." She was a part of the Original Territory comprehended within the precincts of the Original States not only, but also a part of one of those States, and her inhabitants had *joined in the measures* of the

8*

United States in achieving their independence, and she was proposed as a Free State. But such was not the case with Missouri. Hers was a domain alien to the United States at the formation of the Constitution. A district of Territory acquired of a Foreign power since its adoption, and not contemplated in the mutual obligations, guarantees, and concessions contained in the compact of the Ordinance of 1787, or in the provisions of the Constitution. Besides the guarantee of recognition and protection in the ownership of Slave property, which was so peculiar and so sacred between the Original States, there was also, as I have said, the basis of a representation in Congress, apportioned on the Slave-population in the Original States, which could not constitutionally be extended to new and foreign countries by merely purchasing and bringing them within the pale of the Sovereign Jurisdiction of the Union. Whatever their position, as Territories belonging to the New Sovereignty, they could not be admitted, as States, to the enjoyment of these peculiar and exclusive advantages, except by virtue of a new and special compact for their admission thereto. It was competent for the parties to the original compact of the Constitu tion, the Original States, by a new and independent compact for their admission, to guarantee to them the enjoyment of like privileges with themselves; which could not be claimed or conferred *per force* of any Constitutional provision. So also the New Confederacy, now composed of the Original States and the New States admitted into the Federal Alliance with them, might, and must, be parties to such new compact, and that, necessarily, independently of the Constitution. The compact proposed, I repeat, is not with the Original Constitutional Sovereignty of the United States, but with an existing National Sovereignty unknown to the Constitution. And it has reference also to a Territory unknown to the Original Constitutional Jurisdiction, the title to which was derived under no Constitutional provision. Hence the now existing Sovereignty had a right to impose restrictions and exact conditions in the formation of this new compact. They might be willing to give and concede much, and stipulate much, on the subject of taxes, of duties on imports and exports in the proposed New State, of participation in the common benefits of the public domain, of commerce between the States, and in all the advantages of treaties with Foreign powers, the privileges and courtesies of a common citizenship, and a common freedom of intercourse between the Original and the New States now composing the Federal fraternity of States; but to stipulate for the indefinite extension, and the perpetual recognition and protection of involuntary human servitude, involving, as it did, important political relations, was quite another and a different matter. Still, it was necessarily involved in the extension of the National domain beyond the original limits; and although Slavery therein might not claim to be recognized and protected under the Constitution, its recognition and protection might be guaranteed under a new and independent compact. And Slavery might be safe under such a recognition of it in the New State; and the ownership of its Slave property would be abundantly protected under it, so long as the compact should be maintained, by the respective parties to it, in its original integrity and perpetuity.

Hence it was that this Missouri question elicited so much interest, excitement, and agitation, both in and out of Congress.

The vote on the motion of Mr. Roberts, to recommit the Maine Bill, with instructions, after a very exciting debate which lasted for several days, was finally taken in the Senate, on the seventeenth day of January, and the motion was lost; yeas, 18; nays, 25.

The Senate then resumed the consideration of the Bill to admit Maine into the Union, with the reported amendment including Missouri; and Mr. Roberts moved to add to the amendment whereby Missouri was to be admitted to form a State Constitution, the following, viz.—

"*Provided*, that the further introduction into the

said State of persons to be held to Slavery, or involuntary servitude, within the same, shall be absolutely prohibited."

The question on this amendment was debated down to the first day of February, when the vote was taken, and resulted—yeas, 16; nays, 27.

The subject was still further debated in the Senate, on a motion of Mr. Burril, of Rhode Island, to incorporate the first three articles contained in the political compact of the Ordinance of 1787, into the Missouri part of the Maine Bill, in place of the provision which required that the Constitution of Missouri, whenever formed, "shall be republican, and not repugnant to the Constitution of the United States." This motion was withdrawn by the mover, to give place to an amendment proposed by Mr. Thomas, of Illinois, as an additional section to the Missouri part of the Maine Bill, as follows:

"*And be it further enacted*, that in all that tract of country, ceded by France to the United States, under the name of *Louisiana*, which lies north of thirty-six degrees, thirty minutes, North Latitude, excepting only such part thereof as is included within the limits of the State contemplated by this Act, there shall be neither Slavery, nor involuntary servitude, otherwise than in the punishment of crimes whereof the party shall have been duly convicted. *Provided always*, that any person escaping into the same, from whom labor or service is lawfully claimed in any State or Territory of the United States, such fugitive may lawfully be reclaimed, and conveyed to the person claiming his or her labor or service, as aforesaid."

This amendment was subsequently withdrawn by Mr. Thomas, and the debate continued on the proposition to include the two Bills in one Act, as reported by the Judiciary Committee; which was carried in the affirmative, February sixteenth, ayes, 23; noes, 21.

The next day, Mr. Thomas renewed his motion, varying the phraseology so as to make the amendment read—

"*And be it further enacted*, that in all that Territory ceded by France to the United States, under the name of *Louisiana*, which lies north of thirty-six degrees, thirty minutes, North Latitude, excepting only such part thereof as is included within the limits of the State contemplated by this act, Slavery and involuntary servitude, otherwise than in the punishment of crimes whereof the party shall have been duly convicted, shall be, and is hereby, forever prohibited. *Provided always*, that any person escaping into the same, from whom labor or service is lawfully claimed in any State or Territory of the United States, such fugitive may be lawfully reclaimed and conveyed to the person claiming his, or her, labor or service as aforesaid."

This amendment was adopted without debate, yeas 34, nays 10; and after some other alterations to make the different parts of the Bill conformable to each other, the question was taken on ordering the whole Bill, as thus further amended, to be engrossed and read a third time; which resulted, ayes, 34; nays, 20.

The Bill was then ordered to be engrossed and read a third time the next day, Friday, February the eighteenth.

The next day the Bill, entitled, "An Act for the admission of the State of Maine into the Union," was read a third time as amended, the blanks were filled up, and the Bill passed. The title was amended so as to read—" An Act for the admission of the State of Maine into the Union, and to enable the people of Missouri Territory to form a Constitution and State Government, and for the admission of such State into the Union on an equal footing with the Original States; and to prohibit Slavery in certain Territories." Thus far in the Senate.

III.

On the twenty-sixth day of January, 1820, in the House of Representatives, the Bill for the admission of Missouri being under consideration, Mr. Storrs submitted the following by way of amendment, *viz.*—

"*And provided further, and it is hereby enacted*, that, forever hereafter, neither Slavery nor involuntary servitude—except in the punishment of crimes whereof the party shall have been duly convicted—shall exist in the Territory of the United States, lying North of the thirty-eighth degree of North Latitude, and west of the River Mississippi, and the boundaries of the State of Missouri, as established by this Act. *Provided*, that any person escaping into the said Territory, from whom labor or service is lawfully claimed in any of the States, such fugitive may be lawfully reclaimed and conveyed, according to the laws of the United States in such case provided, to the person claiming his, or her, labor or service as aforesaid."

After a desultory debate on the motion, the question was taken, and decided in the negative. The reading of the Bill then proceeded as far as the fourth section, when Mr. Taylor, of New York, proposed to amend by incorporating into that section the following provision, viz.—

Section Fourth, line twenty-fifth, insert after the word States—"And shall ordain and establish that there shall be neither Slavery nor involuntary servitude in the said State, otherwise than in the punishment of crimes whereof the party shall have been duly convicted. *Provided always*, that any person escaping into the same, from whom labor or service is lawfully claimed in any other State, such fugitive may be lawfully reclaimed, and conveyed to the person claiming his or her labor or service as aforesaid. *And provided also*, that the said provision shall not be construed to alter the condition of any person now held to service or labor in the said Territory."

This amendment proposed to make the restriction upon Slavery in the proposed State of Missouri, a part of her State Constitution ; or, in other words, it made the abolition of Slavery in Missouri, a condition of her becoming a State Organization and of her admission into the Union on an equal footing with the Original States. The discussion of this proposition was full, and gave rise to a great deal of acrimonious and fierce debate. It was continued day after day to the nineteenth day of February ensuing, when it assumed another phase by the introduction of the Senate Bill for the admission of Maine and Missouri.

The Senate Bill, it will be remembered, authorized the People of Missouri to form a State Constitution without any restriction upon Slavery, but provided for its restriction by excluding it from the Territory North of thirty-six degrees and thirty minutes North Latitude, and not included in the State limits.

The House now took up this bill from the Senate, and Mr. Taylor, of New York, moved that the amendments of the Senate to the Bill for the admission of Maine, be disagreed to by the House. Mr.

Scott, of Missouri, moved that they be committed to the Committee of the Whole, which then had under consideration the Missouri Bill of the House. The motion of Mr. Scott took precedence of the motion of Mr. Taylor. A long and animated discussion followed, which the reporters hardly attempted to give in detail, and all that is reported is very little else than a statement of the names of those who addressed the House, and of the positions they took on the question before it. Mr. Scott's motion was lost; ayes, 70; nays, 107.

A motion was then made by Mr. Smyth, of Virginia, to lay the amendments of the Senate to the Maine Bill on the table, and to print them, which was lost; and the question recurred on Mr. Taylor's motion to disagree to the amendments of the Senate. During the debate on this motion, the amendment was called *a Compromise*, and some discussion followed as to the fitness of this phraseology. However, the term was appropriated.

Mr. Simkins, of South Carolina, moved that the consideration of the amendments be postponed to Tuesday, February twenty-second; and that they be printed. This motion was carried by a large majority.

On Monday, the twenty-first, the House, in Committee of the whole, resumed the consideration of the Missouri Bill, and the proposed constitutional restriction as to Slavery; which was debated until the hour of adjournment.

On Tuesday, the twenty-second, the Maine and Missouri Bill of the Senate was again taken up, and Mr. Randolph, of Va. delivered a speech upon it, of two hours length, in which he bitterly opposed the restriction contained in the amendment of the Senate, declaring it to be unconstitutional. He was followed by Mr. Rhea, of Tennessee, who gave place to a motion for adjournment, which was carried.

The debate was resumed again on the twenty-third, on the amendments of the Senate to the Maine Bill, now the Maine and Missouri Bill. A division of the House was called for, and on the question—"Will the House disagree to so much of the said amendments as is comprised in the words following, in the Title of the Bill, to wit:—'and to enable the people of Missouri Territory to form a Constitution and State Government, and for the admission of such State into the Union, on an equal footing with the original States,' and 'SECTION II. *And be it further enacted*, that the inhabitants of that portion of the Missouri Territory, included within the boundaries hereinafter designated, be, and they are hereby, authorized to form for themselves a Constitution and State Government, and to assume such name as they shall deem proper.'" The question was carried in the affirmative; the House disagreeing with the amendment of the Senate, which proposed to annex the Missouri Bill to the Maine Bill—yeas, 93; nays, 72.

The question was then taken on disagreeing to the residue of the amendments of the Senate—being the details of the Missouri part of the Bill—with the exception of that which embraced the compromise principle; which was also decided in the affirmative—yeas, 102; nays, 68.

The question was then taken—"Will the House disagree on the said Ninth Section?" being the last of the amendments of the Senate to the Maine Bill, and containing the restrictive clause on the subject of Slavery, north of thirty-six degrees and thirty minutes, North Latitude; which was also determined in the affirmative—for disagreeing 159, against it 18.

Thus the House rejected all the amendments of the Senate to the Bill for the admission of Maine into the Union, which had reference to Missouri.

The Missouri bill was now again taken up. The proposed restriction, for the abolition of Slavery by the State Constitution, being under consideration, Mr. Edwards, of Connecticut, and Mr. Jones, of Tennessee, addressed the House; the former in favor of, the latter against it. The debate was continued from day to day until the twenty-fifth, when Mr. Hill, of Massachusetts, rose, and remarking that the progress of the debate seemed to be stamped with all the marks of eternity, moved, that the Committee of the whole be discharged from any further consideration of the Missouri Bill.

Mr. Lowndes said, if the gentleman from Massachusetts insisted on his motion, he would cheerfully vote for it; but suggested its withdrawal, to give two or three other gentlemen an opportunity to speak to-day; and the motion could be renewed to-morrow if necessary. Whereupon, Mr. Hill withdrew his motion.

Mr. Ervin, of South Carolina, and Mr. Scott, of Missouri, then addressed the House at great length, in opposition to the proposed Slavery restriction. Other gentlemen expressed a wish to be heard on the question, but as the discussion had already been very much protracted, and the public business was suffering, they declined speaking.

Mr. Walker, of North Carolina, attempted to speak, but "the question" was called for "so clamorously and so perseveringly," that he could proceed no further than to move that the Committee rise. The Committee refused to rise, by an almost unanimous vote.

Mr. Smith, of North Carolina, now moved "the previous question." The Speaker, Mr. Clay, conceived the motion to be out of order; and observed that it would not effect the object of the gentleman who moved it. It was then withdrawn; and the question was taken on Mr. Taylor's proposed restriction, and agreed to by from twelve to eighteen majority. Whereupon, on motion, the Committee rose, with leave to sit again, and the House adjourned. 36, *Annals of Congress*, 1540.

On the twenty-sixth of February, Mr. Hill renewed his motion—"That the Committee of the whole be discharged from the further consideration of the Missouri Bill." The motion was lost.

The House then, in Committee of the whole, went into the consideration of the Bill, when Mr. Storrs, of New York, moved to amend it by inserting in the Fourth Section, immediately preceding the restrictive amendment adopted on the twenty-fifth, the following *proviso*, viz.—"That in all that tract of country ceded by France to the United States, under the name of Louisiana, which lies North of thirty-six degrees and thirty minutes, North Latitude, excepting only such part thereof as is included within the limits of the State contemplated by this act, there shall be neither Slavery nor involuntary servitude, otherwise than in the punishment of crimes whereof the party shall have been duly convicted. PROVIDED ALWAYS, that any person escaping into the same from whom labor or service is lawfully claimed in any State or Territory of the United States, such fugitive may be lawfully reclaimed, and conveyed to the person claiming his or her labor or service, as aforesaid."

Mr. Storrs supported this amendment in a speech of considerable length, and was followed by Mr. Randolph, who spoke more than four hours against it. He was followed by Mr. Beecher, of Ohio, who gave way to a motion that the Committee rise, and the House adjourned.

IV.

On Monday, the twenty-eighth of February, the Maine and Missouri Bill of the Senate having been returned to that body on the disagreement of the House upon it, a message was received from the Senate that they insist on their amendments to the Bill for the admission of Maine into the Union.

Mr. Taylor, of New York, moved that the House insist on its disagreement to the said amendments. Mr. Cobb, of Georgia, asked the Chair whether the question could be divided, so as to be taken separately on each principle involved in the amendment.

Mr. Lowndes, of South Carolina, remarked that it appeared to him that there would be much difficulty in coming to any conclusion on these amendments, in which the two Houses would concur. He thought, therefore, that it would be better to lay them aside, until the House had matured and finally acted on the Bill before it for the admission of Missouri, and should ascertain how it was received by the Senate. With this view, he moved that the amendments be laid on the table. On this question the House divided, and the motion was lost—ayes, 74; nays, 85.

Mr. Culpeper, of North Carolina, then urged the necessity and propriety of mutual forbearance on a question so important and delicate. With the hope that by acting conclusively on the Bill now before the House for the admission of Missouri, and sending it to the Senate, all difficulty would be gotten over, he moved that the consideration of the amendments be postponed till to-morrow—February twenty-ninth.

This motion was opposed by Mr. Holmes, and by Mr. Whitman, of Mass.; on the ground that they were averse to delaying a final decision on the amendments with which the admission of Maine was connected, and which they wished to separate from it as promptly as possible. Whereupon the motion to postpone the consideration of the amendments was put and lost, without a count.

The main question then recurring, it was so divided, on motion of Mr. Butler, of Louisiana, as to be first taken on insisting on the disagreement of the House to the first Eight Sections, connecting with the Bill for the admission of Maine the Bill for the admission of Missouri. The House insisted on their disagreement; ayes, 97; nays, 76.

The question was then taken on the disagreement

of the House to the remaining amendment of the Senate, contained in the Ninth Section, and embracing the restriction upon Slavery, which was now called *the compromise principle.*

Mr. Lowndes, of South Carolina, wished simply to remark, before the question was taken, that although he should always be ready to vote for such a proposition substantially, when presented to him combined with the free admission of Missouri; yet as the amendment relative to Missouri had been disagreed to, it would be useless to retain this amendment in connection with the Maine Bill alone, and as, therefore, he should now vote against retaining it, he wished his motive to be understood.

Mr. McCreary, of South Carolina, remarked to the same effect. The question was now put, on the House insisting on its disagreement to the Ninth Section of the Senate's amendment to the Maine Bill, and was carried, ayes, 160; nays, 14.

So the House again disagreed to the whole of the Senate's amendment to the Bill for the admission of Maine, and directed the clerk so to inform the Senate. The Senate then asked a conference on the subject, and informed the House that they had appointed Managers for that purpose, on their part.

The House now went into Committee of the whole, Mr. Cobb, of Georgia, being in the chair, on the Missouri Bill. Mr. Storrs' motion to insert therein the clause excluding Slavery from the Territory west of the Mississippi, and north of thirty-six degrees and thirty minutes, North Latitude, being still under consideration,

Mr. Beecher, of Ohio, resumed and concluded his speech against it, and advocated the right of Congress to impose the Slavery restriction heretofore discussed, upon the State of Missouri, as a condition of her admission into the Union, as proposed.

Mr. Randolph, of Virginia, addressed the House at great length against the amendment offered by Mr. Storrs, as also against any restriction, and against the argument of Mr. Beecher.

Mr. Mallory, of Vermont, would vote against the amendment, though he was in favor of restriction in the Territories west of the Mississippi.

Mr. Storrs, then, again addressed the Committee in a brief but earnest speech in favor of his proposition.

Mr. Livermore, of New Hampshire, was opposed to the amendment; and in favor of the State restriction.

Mr. Baldwin, of Pennsylvania, spoke in favor of the amendment and also in reply to one or two points raised by Mr. Beecher. The question was put on Mr. Storrs' amendment, which was lost. Sundry other amendments were then successively suggested, and either rejected or withdrawn ; one of which, made by

Mr. Storrs, proposed to modify the restrictive clause already adopted, so as to make it a recommendation, for the acceptance or rejection of the Convention of Missouri as an article of compact, to exclude Slavery in the State Constitution instead of requiring it as an absolute condition of her admission. Thus the subject stood at the hour of adjournment.

On Tuesday, the twenty-ninth day of February, the House proceeded to consider the Message from the Senate, asking a conference upon the subject of the discordant action of the two Houses on the amendments of the Senate to the Bill for the admission of Maine. Whereupon it was—

Resolved, That this House do agree to the conference asked by the Senate, upon the subject matter of the disagreeing votes of the two Houses on the amendments depending to the Bill aforesaid; and that Managers be appointed to the same on their part.

Ordered, That Mr. Holmes, Mr. Taylor, Mr. Lowndes, Mr. Parker, of Massachusetts, and Mr. Kinsley, be Managers on the part of the House.

The House then took up The Missouri Bill, authorising the people of the Territory of Missouri to form a Constitution and State Government; and proceeded to consider the amendments reported by the Committee, which being read, were concurred in with the exception of the following:—"And shall ordain and establish, that there shall be neither Slavery, nor involuntary servitude in the said State, otherwise than in the punishment of crimes, whereof the party shall have been duly convicted. *Provided always*, that any person escaping within the same, from whom labour or service is lawfully claimed in any other State, such fugitive may be lawfully reclaimed, and conveyed to the person claiming his, or her, labour or service, as aforesaid. *Provided nevertheless*, that the said provision shall not be construed to alter the condition, or civil rights of any person now held to service or labour in said Territory."

The question was stated, to concur in this amendment, when Mr. Storrs, moved to amend by striking out the words " and shall ordain and establish that," and in lieu thereof to insert—" *and be it further enacted*, that the following propositions be, and the same are hereby offered to the said Convention for their free acceptance, or rejection, to be incorporated into the Constitution of the said State, as articles of compact between the said States and the United States, viz.: that there be neither Slavery nor involuntary servitude," etc., following the words of the Committee's amendment. After some debate on this motion it was lost; ayes, 82; nays, 98.

The question was then taken on the restrictive amendment reported by the Committee, on the motion of Mr. Taylor, and was decided in the affirmative, ayes, 94; nays, 86.

Mr. Taylor then renewed a motion made by him unsuccessfully in Committee of the whole, to amend the last section of the Bill, by striking out the words "and the said States, when formed, shall be admitted into the Union on an equal footing with the Original States," and insert in lieu thereof—"and if the same" Constitution "shall be approved by Congress, the said Territory shall be admitted into the Union as a State, upon an equal footing with the Original States." Which was lost, ayes, 49; nays, 125.

The question was now taken upon ordering the Bill to be engrossed and read a third time, which was carried; so the Bill was ordered to be engrossed and read a third time on the morrow, March first. Ayes, 93; nays, 84.

House of Representatives, Wednesday, March first, 1820. The Engrossed Bill was read a third time, and the question put, "Shall this Bill pass?"

Mr. Randolph rose and spoke more than three hours against the passage of the Bill, opposing the proposed restrictive Slavery clause as unconstitutional and unjust. When he concluded, Mr. Holmes, of Massachusetts, called for the previous question, and the House sustained the call; whereupon the main question was taken on the final passage of the Bill, and decided in the affirmative, ayes, 91; noes, 82.

The Bill was then sent to the Senate for their concurrence, and the House adjourned.

Thursday, March second. A message was received from the Senate, informing the House that the Senate had passed the Missouri Bill, with an amendment; which amendment was, to strike out the Slavery restriction upon the State, and insert instead thereof, the clause—Mr. Thomas' and Mr. Storrs' orig inal proposition to exclude Slavery from all the Territories of the United States, west of the Mississippi, and north of thirty-six degrees and thirty minutes North Latitude, except within the limits of the proposed State of Missouri.

On motion of Mr. Holmes, this Message from the Senate was laid on the table, to enable him to make a report from the Committee of Conference on the Maine and Missouri Bill of the Senate; Whereupon Mr. Holmes, from the Managers appointed on the part of the House to confer with the Managers on the part of the Senate, upon the subject-matter of the discordance of the two Houses on the amendments of the Senate to the Bill of the House, entitled "An Act providing for the admission of the State of Maine into the Union," made the following report as a compromise.

FIRST. They recommend to the Senate, to recede from their amendments to the said Bill.

SECOND. They recommend to the two Houses to agree to strike out the fourth section of the Bill from the House of Representatives, now pending in the Senate, entitled—"An Act to authorize the people of Missouri to form a Constitution and State Government, and for the admission of such State into the Union, on an equal footing with the Original States," the following proviso in the following words: "and shall ordain and establish that there shall be neither Slavery nor involuntary servitude in said State, otherwise than in the punishment of crimes whereof the party shall have been duly convicted. PROVIDED ALWAYS, that any person escaping into the same, from whom labour or service is lawfully claimed in any other State, such fugitive may be lawfully reclaimed and conveyed to the person claiming his, or her service as aforesaid; PROVIDED NEVERTHELESS that the said provision shall not be construed to alter the condition, or civil rights, of any person now held to service or labor in said Territory."

And that the following provision be added to the Bill.

"SECTION EIGHTH. *And be it further enacted*, that in all that Territory ceded by France to the United States, under the name of Louisiana, which lies north of thirty-six degrees and thirty minutes North Latitude, not included within the limits of the State contemplated by this Act, Slavery and involuntary servitude, otherwise than in the punishment of crimes whereof the party shall have been duly convicted, shall be, and is hereby, forever prohibited. PROVIDED ALWAYS, that any person escaping into the same, from whom labor or service is lawfully claimed in any other State or Territory of the United States, such fugitive may be lawfully reclaimed, and conveyed to the person claiming his or her labor or service."

The Report being read, was laid on the table; and the House resumed the consideration of the Amendments of the Senate to the Missouri Bill, upon which the question was divided so as to be first taken on striking out the Slavery restriction upon the State of Missouri.

Mr. Lowndes, of South Carolina, spoke briefly, and advocated the compromise recommended by the Committee of Conference; and urged with great earnestness the propriety of a decision which would restore tranquility to the country: which, he said, was demanded by every consideration of moderation, of wisdom, and of virtue.

Mr. Holmes, of Massachusetts, spoke to the same effect.

Mr. Adams, of Massachusetts, spoke in favor of the State restriction and against the Compromise.

Mr. Kinsey, of New Jersey, Mr. Stephens, of Connecticut, and Mr. Mercer, of Virginia, each spoke in favor of the Compromise, when the previous question was called, and the call being sustained by the

House, the question was taken on concurring with the Senate in striking out of the Bill the Slavery restriction on the State of Missouri, and decided in the affirmative, ayes 90, nays 87.

The question was then stated upon the second part of the amendment of the Senate, when Mr. Taylor moved to amend the amendment of the Senate, by striking out the words, "thirty-six degrees and thirty minutes, North Latitude," and to insert a line which would exclude Slavery from all the Territory West of the Mississippi River, except Louisiana, Missouri, and Arkansas.

The previous question being demanded and sustained by the House, Mr. Taylor's motion was excluded, and the main question was then stated on concurring with the Senate in inserting in the Bill, in place of the Slavery restriction on the proposed State of Missouri, the clause prohibiting Slavery in the Territory north of thirty-six degrees and thirty minutes, North Latitude: which was decided in the affirmative, ayes, 134; nays, 42.

The amendment made to the Title of the Bill, by adding the words—"and to prohibit Slavery in certain Territories," was then concurred in, which made the whole Title to read—"An Act to authorize the people of the Missouri Territory to form a Constitution and State Government, and for the admission of such State into the Union on an equal footing with

10*

the Original States, and to prohibit Slavery in certain Territories." All the amendments being thus concurred in, the Bill was passed by both Houses. See the Bill. 3, *U. S. Stat. at large*, 545.

On the twenty-second day of February, 1821, on motion of Henry Clay, a Committee on the part of the House was appointed, to join a Committe on the part of the Senate, on the subject of the admission of Missouri under the State Constitution formed pursuant to the provisions of the aforesaid Act. On the twenty-sixth of the same month, Mr. Clay, from the Joint Committee, reported a resolution for the admission of Missouri "upon the fundamental condition that the Fourth Clause of the Twenty-Sixth Section of the Third Article of the Constitution submitted on the part of the said State to Congress, shall never be construed to authorize the passage of any law, and that no law shall be passed in conformity thereto, by which any citizen of either of the States in this Union, shall be excluded from the enjoyment of any of the privileges and immunities to which such citizen is entitled under the Constitution of the United States. *Provided*, that the Legtslature of the said State, by a solemn Public Act, shall declare the assent of the said State to the said fundamental condition, and shall transmit to the President of the United States, on or before the Fourth day of November next, an authentic copy of the said Act, upon the receipt whereof the President, by Proclamation, shall announce the fact; whereupon, and without any further proceeding on the part of Congress, the admission of the said State into this Union shall be considered as complete." 3, *U. S. Stat. at large*, 653.

That section of the Constitution of Missouri, referred to in the foregoing Resolution, was as follows, viz.:—"The General Assembly shall have power to pass Laws—to permit the owners of Slaves to emancipate them, saving the rights of creditors, where the person so emancipating will give security that the slave so emancipated shall not become a public charge. It shall be their duty as soon as may be, to pass such laws as may be necessary;

FIRST. To prevent free negroes and mulattoes from coming to, and settling in this State, under any pretext whatsoever. And,

SECOND. To oblige the owners of Slaves to treat them with humanity, and to abstain from all injuries to them, extending to life and limb." *Revised Statutes of Missouri*, 32, 33.

The power of the National Sovereignty to impose restrictions upon the Constitution even, of a New State, before its actual admission into the Union, is very forcibly illustrated in this resolution. The condition therein provided, was accepted by the Legislature of Missouri by "A Solemn Public Act, declaring the assent of the State to this fundamental condition," which Act was approved by the Governor of Missouri

June twenty-sixth, 1821. The President of the United States, issued his Proclamation, declaring the actual admission of Missouri into the Union as a State, on the twentieth day of August, in the same year: and on the sixteenth day of March, 1822, the Laws of the United States were duly extended over the State of Missouri, by Act of Congress.

Such was the compact under which the New National Sovereignty of the United States consented to relinquish its supremacy over the Missouri Territory so far as to enable the people inhabiting therein to erect themselves into a State, with the same rights of freedom, sovereignty, and independence as the other States, and to form a State Constitution, with a view to their admission into the Union as a Slave State, "on an equal footing with the Original States." Such was the origin and the nature of the Missouri Compromise. It was predicated upon the absence of any power in Congress, under the Constitution, to extend or recognize Slavery beyond the limits of the Original State and Territorial domain of the United States. It was a compact for the extension of Slavery on the one hand, and for its restriction on the other; for its recognition and protection in the State of Missouri, and its perpetual abolition, or exclusion, beyond the line of thirty-six degrees and thirty minutes, North Latitude. Thus the whole country purchased from France by the United States under the name of Louisiana,—except as provided in the Eighth Section of this Compact—was interdicted to freedom and opened to the occupancy of Slavery; and as a consideration or compensation for all this concession to it, its perpetual prohibition beyond that line was guaranteed by the National Sovereignty.

The Compact was an important one. It was as important to humanity and to freedom as was the Compact of the Ordinance of 1787, or even of the Constitution itself. It was all the more important because it was unconstitutional. Otherwise it needed not to have been made the subject of compromise. The proviso in favor of the recaption of fugitive slaves, stands a recorded admission of its unconstitutionality. It stands an admission that Slavery in Missouri, and in the New Territory purchased from France, was beyond the reach of any Constitutional recognition or protection. For what need of the proviso, if the government, under the Constitution, could recognise the existence of Slavery, and protect the ownership of Slave property, in that newly acquired domain?

What need of such a proviso, if the admission into the Union "on an equal footing with the Original States in all respects whatever," brought the ownership of Slave property therein, within the protection of the Constitutional provision for the reclamation of fugitives from service? Indeed, what need was there for any provision for the reclamation of Fugitive Slaves escaping from the Original States into the said Territory, if the Constitutional provision was ample and sufficient for this purpose? I say again, the very existence of this proviso is a recorded admission that Slavery was not, and could not be, recognised or protected there under the Constitution. Hence, I repeat again, hence the necessity of a New Compact for it, independently of the Constitution. The Compact therefore is the basis of the recognition and protection given to Slavery in this new domain; And so long as the Compact stands, whether it is Constitutional or not, so long must the National Sovereignty recognize and protect it, and just so long is its power sufficient to recognize and protect it, within the limits of its provisions.

The clear legal inference from all these premises is this. The regulation or government of Foreign Territory added to the National domain since the adoption of the Constitution; and the admission into the Union of States formed out of such Territory, are not comprehended in its provisions. The recognition of Slavery, or the protection of property in Slaves, in such States or Territory, therefore, is not a subject of Constitutional regulation, but of compact between the several States composing the National Sovereignty, and the people inhabiting in the New Territory, at the time of its acquisition; or in the proposed New State at the time of its admission. Hence, if a State is proposed to be created out of such Territory, with a view to be admitted into the general Union, it is done not by virtue of any original Constitutional provision, but must be done by virtue of a New Compact, made between the States which, as members of the General Union, were parties to the acquisition; and the people of the State or Territory proposed to be admitted. This Compact may, it must, prescribe and determine the conditions and terms upon which such New State may be created, as also of its admission. If it does not recognize the existence of Slavery, or guarantee protection to the ownership of Slave property, in the proposed New State, under the laws of the United States, it is not recognized there, and cannot be protected there under the Constitutional provision, or by virtue of any Law of Congress made in pursuance thereof.

It is true, nevertheless, that the people of the Slave holding States have a right,—not indeed under the Constitution, and therefore not a Constitutional right, but,—under the Compact of purchase to which they were parties, to go with their Slave property into the newly acquired Territory. But this right of transmigration or of occupancy does not, of necessity, give them a right to have it recognized there by the National Government so as to become the basis of a representation in Congress, or so as to guarantee their ownership of it there under the Constitution, as in the Original States. Such a recognition of it there, and the right of reclamation in case of its escape, must be the subject of especial compact with the National Sovereignty, bringing it within its jurisdiction, as in the Missouri Compromise Compact: And by virtue of the same power it may also prohibit it. In this originates the true and only National recognition of Slavery, and the guarantee of protection given to the ownership of Slave property, where it enters upon Territory not comprehended within the limits of the Original Constitutional jurisdiction of the United States.

Hence we see the importance to Slavery of the Compromise provision in the Compact for the admission of Missouri into the Union as a Slave State. Its perpetuity was as important to the Slave States as it was to the Free States. It was more so, for freedom was thereby more restricted than Slavery. The first proposition was, to require of Missouri as a condition of her being erected into a State Organization, and of her admission into the Union as such, to provide in her State Constitution for the abolition of Slavery within her precincts. The Compromise was, to relinquish this exaction on condition that Slavery should, by the common consent of all the parties to the Compact, be forever prohibited in, or excluded from the rest of the said Territory, as in the Eighth Section of the Act. It was a compact made by the people of all the States then composing the National Sovereignty, with each other, and with the people of the proposed State of Missouri, and the people who should thereafter inhabit in the said Territory, precisely similar to the Compact contained in the Ordinance of 1787. Every section of it was as much and as truly and really binding upon the parties to it as the whole was; and each distinct section just as much so as any and every other. The subject of it was a matter of universal and not merely sectional interest; of perpetual and not merely temporary obligation: And it was thus settled at this time, by those who understood the subject, and looked at and considered it in all its comprehensive sequences and relations.

The settlement of it brought repose to the Country, strengthened the bonds of fraternity and union between the States, and inspired the hope that the result might be—as was predicted by the advocates of Slavery-extension—the improvement of the condition of the Slave population, and the gradual decrease of Slavery itself, by dispersing it over a broader surface without any other source of supply than its natural increase. The argument, both on the score of humanity and expediency in this regard, was urged by such men as Henry Clay, James Madison, Thomas Jefferson, and others, and was at least plausible.

This was the second great National Era of Slavery in the United States. For long years subsequent to this period the question of its further recognition and extension was at rest, and continued to be at rest until there came another era in our history which made it again a question of quite as much national interest and importance. This too, was a contingency not anticipated, and therefore not provided for, by the framers of the Constitution. It was the admission into the Federal Union of an already independent and Sovereign Republic, owing no allegiance to, and never having sustained any ties of political dependence upon, the United States. I mean the Annexation of Texas.

V.

The principle of a Sovereignty in the National Government derived independently and outside of the Constitution, was very forcibly and aptly illustrated in the Annexation of Texas to the United States by a joint resolution of Congress, in 1845. The Sovereignty, called the United States, was at this time composed of the Thirteen Original States; the New States of Vermont, Maine, Indiana, Illinois, Ohio, Michigan, Mississippi, Alabama, Kentucky, and Tennessee, formed out of the Original Territorial domain known to the Constitution, and within the boundaries of the United States as settled by the Treaty with Great Britain ; and the New States of Louisiana, Missouri, Arkansas and Florida, four State Organizations created out of Territory foreign to the Original States and not known to the Constitution, or recognized as within its original jurisdiction. The domain and Sovereignty over the latter, Florida, was purchased by the then United States, from Spain, February twenty-second, 1819.

Here again, we have a New National Sovereignty vastly different from that established under the Constitution—different in the extent of its domain, in the reach of its jurisdiction, and in the source of its supremacy. In its Federal and State relations, nevertheless, it is the Constitution still which limits both its Sovereignty and the Allegiance which is its due: While in its Territorial possessions, its own inherent or purchased Sovereignty is the source of its supremacy. It was in the exercise of its Sovereign right to acquire Territory outside of the Constitution, that this New Sovereignty, called the United States, resolved upon the Annexation of Texas. The Act cannot be defended or sustained on any other theory. It was as foreign to and as independent of any provision contained in the Constitution, or any power given to Congress therein, as was the Treaty of Peace with Great Britain in 1783. It certainly cannot be claimed that there is any provision in the Constitution for any such anomalous proceeding. Suppose, in the phraseology of the same Resolution, it should be to-day—RESOLVED *by the Senate and House of Representatives of the United States of America, in Congress assembled,* That Congress doth consent that the Kingdom of Great Britain may be erected into a New State to be called the State of Great Britain, with a Republican form of Government, to be adopted by the people thereof, by deputies in Convention assembled, with the consent of the existing Government, in order that the same may be admitted as one of the States of this Union,"—would any one contend that this resolution was in pursuance of any provision, or authority for it, contained in the Constitution? Certainly not. And how was it different with Texas? What provision in the Constitution is it under which her admission into the Union as an Original Member of the Confederated Republic is provided for? And then look at the conditions upon which such consent of Congress was predicated. Well enough indeed, when referred to simply in connection with the one grand purpose of the enactment, the transfer of her domain and Sovereignty to the United States, but hardly sufficient to bring her into the Union "on an equal footing with the Original

States" as to the subject of Slavery, under the Constitution.

One of the provisions contained in the Compact, under which the consent of Congress was given to her being erected into a State, with a view to her admission, specifies—

"THIRD. New States of convenient size, not exceeding four in number, in addition to said State of Texas, and having sufficient population, may hereafter, by the consent of the said State, be formed out of the Territory thereof, which shall be entitled to admission under the provisions of the Federal Constitution: And such States as may be formed out of that portion of said Territory lying South of thirty-six degrees and thirty minutes, North Latitude, commonly known as the Missouri Compromise Line, shall be admitted into the Union *with or without Slavery* as the people of each State asking admission may desire: and in such State or States as shall be formed out of said Territory North of said Missouri Compromise Line, Slavery, or involuntary servitude, (except for crimes) shall be prohibited."

Now, I ask, what power has Congress, under the Constitution, to make any such provision for the admission into the Union of an Independent Sovereign power, or of New States formed, or to be formed, out of its Territory? Clearly none. This very section concedes that no such power is given by the Constitution. Else whence and why this new provision for the admission of such New States? If the admission of the Republic of Texas into the Union "on an equal footing with the Original States in all respects whatever," was constitutional, and that stipulation placed her and her Territorial domain under all the provisions of the Constitution, in the same sense and to the same extent as the Original States were under them, where was the need of any new provision for the admission of any New State, comprehended within her Territorial limits? And what provision of the Constitution can be made, under any just rule of construction, to sustain these stipulations on the subject of Slavery? Certainly none, certainly the Constitution was never intended to give such a limitless recognition to Slavery, or so immeasurably to extend it, and that too over Territory whence Congress, acting under it, had already prohibited its importation. It cannot be.

Still I do not mean for one moment to question, nay rather my argument is, that it was competent for the United States composing the Federal Union when Texas was admitted, to make just such a Compact, independently of the Constitution. But I deny that, after it is made, Slavery can be recognized or sustained there under the Constitution, independently of the Compact. The United States, acting in their New Sovereign Capacity, may stipulate to extend the provisions of the Federal Constitution and the Laws made in pursuance thereof, over Texas for any and all purposes whatsoever, but it is a stipulation made independently of the Constitution itself. The Compact, it must be remembered, is a Compact between two distinct and Independent Sovereignties. Neither of them known originally to the Constitution. One of them the Republic of Texas, the other the enlarged Republic of the United States. It was a Compact for the sale and transfer of the former to the supremacy and jurisdiction of the latter, so as to give to it the position of membership in the General Union, while it retained just so much and no more of its independency than was necessary to give it the position of a distinct State Organization in the Federal Fraternity of States. The Constitution had no more to do with the Compact on the part of the United States, than it had to do with the Compact on the part of the Republic of Texas. It has no provision in it which prescribes or specifies the terms which shall be dictated by the former, any more than it does the mode of approach which shall be pursued by the latter. Both are acting in their Sovereign capacity, and independently of any power derived under the provisions of the Constitution.

The joint resolution for the Annexation of the

Republic of Texas to the United States, was passed and approved March First, 1845. The joint resolution of Congress for the admission of the State of Texas into the Union, pursuant to the provisions of the Compact contained in the former resolution, was approved December Twenty-ninth, 1845, and was as follows, viz.:

"WHEREAS, the Congress of the United States, by a joint resolution, approved March the First, eighteen hundred and forty-five, did consent that the Territory properly included within, and rightfully belonging to, the Republic of Texas, might be erected into a New State, to be called the State of Texas, with a Republican form of Government to be adopted by the people of said Republic, by deputies in Convention assembled, with the consent of the existing Government, in order that the same might be admitted as one of the States of this Union; which consent of Congress was given upon certain conditions specified in the First and Second Sections of said joint resolution—AND WHEREAS, the people of the said Republic of Texas, by deputies in Convention assembled, with the consent of the existing government, did adopt a Constitution, and erect a New State with a Republican form of Government, and, in the name of the people of Texas, and by their authority, did ordain and declare that they assented to, and accepted, the proposals, conditions, and guarantees contained in said First and Second sections of said resolution.—AND WHEREAS, the said Constitution, and the proper evidence of its adoption by the people of the Republic of Texas, have been transmitted to the President of the United States, and laid before Congress, in conformity to the provisions of the said joint resolution ; THEREFORE,

"RESOLVED, by the Senate and House of Representatives of the United States of America, in Congress assembled, That the State of Texas shall be one, and is hereby declared to be one of the United States of America, and admitted into the Union on an equal footing with the Original States, in all respects whatsoever."

Did this resolution admit Texas into the Union so as Constitutionally to legalize the Compact made with her in regard to Slavery, under which the consent of Congress was given to her forming a Constitution and State Government with a view to her admission ? Certainly it could not, for no one of the Original States stood on any such footing under the Constitution. There was no provision in it with reference to them, and there was no Compact between the Original States themselves, which contemplated the admission of States into the Union "either with or without Slavery, as the people of each State (Territory) asking admission may desire."

The people inhabiting in the State or Territory of Texas cannot certainly claim, under this resolution, any greater advantages for Slavery than were accorded to it in the Original States under the Constitution. The question then necessarily arises, how far is Slavery recognized and protected in Texas, or in any part of the Territorial domain which belonged to her as an Independent Republic, under the Compact for her admission? No farther, certainly, than the Compact of surrender or annexation, and admission, itself provides: and only under that Compact; and not by virtue of any provision in the Constitution independent of the Compact. The Compact is therefore the true and only basis and the limit of its recognition by the General Government. If it is asked that her representation in Congress be apportioned on a Slave population as in the Original States, it must be conceded under the Compact for her annexation and admission, though it could not be under the Constitution. If it is asked as to the right to reclaim fugitives from labor or service that the people inhabiting in her Territory may be placed on the same footing with the Original States, it is conceded by virtue of the Compact, though it may not be under the Constitution. But to be on the same footing with the Original States in this respect—and more than this cannot be claimed—the places of escape and of refuge must be the same to which the

Original States were restricted under the Constitution. Beyond that, and within her State or Territorial limits, Slave property must be recognized and protected, if at all, not by the Constitution, but by the Compact between herself and the United States on her annexation or admission. If that Compact fails, or is repudiated as unconstitutional, or because unconstitutional, then Slavery is unrecognized, and the ownership of Slave property is unprotected, within her State and Territorial precincts, by any authority of the United States whatsoever.

But again, and farther. The Compact with Texas being made with her in her Sovereign capacity, cannot be construed as if it were made with a Territory originally or already a part of the public domain of the United States, that might by possibility give the people inhabiting therein some equitable claim to admission into the Union with Slavery. But the parties contracting are perfectly independent of each other in all respects whatsoever. And what are they contracting about? A. and B. are contracting with each other for the sale and purchase of a certain tract of land belonging to A. A. stipulates, on certain precedent conditions, that he will sell the land to B. Now the agreement to sell may be one thing, and the actual sale may be another and a very different thing. The conditions of the agreement to sell, or to purchase, may be quite other and different from the terms of the sale and the purchase itself: So here; the United States agree that on her complying with certain precedent conditions, they will consent that a part of the Territory of Texas, an Independent Sovereignty, may be erected into a New State, in order that as such State—not as such Independent and Sovereign Republic—she may apply for admission into the Union: Now all the while she is performing these precedent conditions, whether called an Independent Republic or a New State, Texas is acting in her own Sovereign capacity; independent both of Congress and the Constitution. The conditions upon which assent is given by Congress, or the National Sovereignty of the United States, to these preliminary proceedings on her part, are one thing: The Compact for her actual admission into the Union is, or may be, quite another thing. Her admission as such New State into the Union is another Compact than that which relates to the conditions precedent to her becoming such a State Organization, viz.; the surrender of a portion of her domain, and her Sovereignty as an Independent Republic, to the United States. That was her own act. It required no enabling Act of Congress to give her power or permission thus to change her political character or condition. She was already Independent and Sovereign, and in the exercise of her own Sovereignty could have made herself a

State in the sense of the Constitution of the United States, without thereby becoming entitled to admission into the Union. But something more was necessary. She could not force herself into the Union. The proposition on her part was, to renounce her political character of an independent and Sovereign Nation, to surrender a portion of her domain and her Sovereignty, and to assume the position of a State Organization whose Sovereignty must necessarily be subject to the higher Sovereignty of the United States, agreeably to the principles of the Federal Constitution. So that the one Compact was an agreement, or treaty, with her in her Sovereign capacity independent of the Constitution; the other a Compact with her as a political organization whose imperial or exclusive Sovereignty was surrendered to the Sovereign jurisdiction of the United States: That is, to the jurisdiction of a Sovereignty other than that created by the Constitution. She calls herself no more a Nation, but a State. She surrenders a part of her Territory, and puts herself on the same level as to her political character with the Original States, and then, by virtue of the Compact for her annexation or admission made with this New Sovereignty, the United States, and not *per force* of any Constitutional provision, she is admitted into Union with the other States, with the same and no more rights of freedom, Sovereignty and

Independence. Hence it follows that the institution of Slavery cannot be recognized or protected in the State or Territory of Texas under the Constitution, independently of this Compact. To thus recognize and protect it there would be to place her beyond the footing of the Original States. They were prohibited exporting Slaves from the United States into such Foreign Territory as Texas then was, and also from bringing them from such Territory into the United States: And can Congress, under the Constitution, and in the face of the Laws of the United States, made in pursuance thereof, thus import Slavery and place it on a better footing than it stood in the Original States? It may indeed pass new or extend existing laws over her Territory, now its own property, for the protective recognition of Slavery, in pursuance of the Compact with Texas before she became a member of, or upon her admission into, the Union; and those laws would be valid and effective so lo ng as the National Government recognizes the validity of the Compact upon which they are based. But repeal that Compact, or pronounce it void, or once insist that it need not be abided by because it is a Compact outside of the Constitution, however sacred it may be, and the recognition of Slavery and the protection guaranteed to Slave property in the Sate or Territory of Texas, by the laws of the United States, is forever at an end.

But this Compact with Texas not only extends, it also guarantees the integrity of, the Missouri Compact: It provides for the formation of a certain number of Slave States out of that portion of the Territory of Texas lying South of the Missouri Compromise Line, and prohibits Slavery in such States as may be formed out of the Territory lying North of that line. The one provision guarantees the extension and protection of Slavery, the other restricts and prohibits it. If the Compact for its restriction is void because unconstitutional, or because made outside of the Constitution; so also is the Compact for its extension and protection void for the same reason. This Compact, as I have shown, is just as unconstitutional as the Compact with Missouri, called the Missouri Compromise: Indeed in principle it is one and the same thing. It re-enacts and extends the Missouri restriction upon Slavery. And if Congress may rightfully repeal the latter Compact on the bare ground that there is no provision for it in the Constitution, it may upon the same principle repeal the other. Whether then in the Texas Territory or the Missouri Territory, on the South of this line freedom is restricted, on the North of it Slavery is restricted. If you remove the restriction upon Slavery on the one side, you also remove the restriction upon freedom on the other side: and freedom becomes freer on both sides.

VI.

I call this the third great National Era of Slavery in the United States. There is yet another, and one still more novel and interesting, and alike unprovided for in the Constitution. This too, originated in a contingency unforeseen by the framers of the Constitution. Not only so, but in a contingency not even anticipated by the framers of the Missouri Compact, nor by those who promoted the annexation and admission of Texas. Hardly dreamed of by any man living in the United States when Texas was admitted into the Union. I mean the acquisi tion of Foreign Territory, and the enlargement of the National domain and Sovereignty of the United States, by conquest: By the war with Mexico. Certainly it will not be claimed that the Constitution provided for any such contingency. True, it gives to Congress power to declare war, but this was only declaratory of the power of Congress in exclusion of the States. It is well known that the great aim and interest of our National Sovereignty at that time was, to be at peace with all the world. We were in fact at amity with all the Nations of Europe, and especially with that Power which held the Sovereignty in Mexico. Of course the framers of the Constitution did not anticipate, or make any special provision in anticipation of, or with reference to, any such emergency; certainly not as regarded Slavery.

Hence again, on the acquisition of this New Territory the question of the extension and restriction of Slavery became one of National interest and importance. It affected anew the character of our National Sovereignty, the powers of Congress, and the relations of the States. Every State and the people of every State in the Union were deeply and rightfully alive to the issue thus again originated. Now too, it was a question of more than ordinary National interest and importance. This vast and exuberant domain, rich in its mineral, agricultural and commercial resources, now for the first time since the discovery of America opened to the entrance of a Protestant Christianity, with all its elements of political and religious freedom, individual elevation, and social advancement, was deservedly an object of deep and thrilling interest and attention to the people of the United States in all parts of the Union. It was an object of interest to the Slave as well as to the Free States. Each by virtue of its membership in the Federal Fraternity, and its title to share in the benefits of the common acquisition, had a proprietary right in the question of its government and its occupancy. As matters now stood in the United States, the Slave-holding States as well as the Free States were entitled to a fair consideration in the settlement as well as the Government of this newly acquired domain. Not—as I have said—

by virtue of any Constitutional provision prescribing or defining the recognition to be given to the ownership of Slave property—but by virtue of their being parties to the conflict, and participating in the struggle, and contributing by men, money, and other measures, to its acquisition: Or, as the framers of the Constitution would have expressed it, by virtue of their being "members of the Union, and joining in the measures of the United States" to prosecute the war and make the conquest.

The Constitution could do nothing for them in this respect: Congress could do nothing for them in pursuance of any power derived under the Constitution: Compact, Compromise, must do all that could be done. The whole policy of the Goverument from its first formation, the Constitution, and the laws made in pursuance of it, all were against the further extension of Slavery, against the restriction of freedom. Still, it must be conceded that the people of the Slave States were equitably entitled to ask that this newly acquired Territory should be opened to the entrance of their Slave property, so far as the National Sovereignty was concerned; and that being conceded, to a just recognition and protection of it.

Hence originated the Compromise Measures of Eighteen hundred and fifty. These were the same in theory with those of eighteen hundred and twenty and eighteen hundred and forty-five. They were based on the same principles, and cannot be sustained on any other. So far as they go to extend or to recognize Slavery, or to provide for its after extension in any portion of that Territory, or to give it a protective or political recognition there under the laws of the United States; to make any part of it either a place of ownership and escape, or of refuge and recaption; or to enforce the right of reclamation within its precincts; or to make it a ratio of representation in Congress; so far they are founded on a Compact originating outside of the Constitution: A Compact made by the National Sovereignty independently of the Constitution, and they can neither give or insure to Slavery any recognition or protection under the Constitution or laws of the United States independently of that Compact or Compromise.

The Fugitive Slave Law, so called, of September, eighteen hundred and fifty, purports to be, and is entitled "An Act to amend and supplementary to, An Act entitled, 'An Act respecting fugitives from justice and persons escaping from the service of their Masters, approved February twelfth, one thousand seven hundred and ninety-three.'"

The Sixth Section of this supplementary Act provides—"*And be it further enacted, etc.;*—that when a person held to service or labor in any State or Territory of the United States, has heretofore, or shall hereafter, escape into another State or Territory, of the United States, the person or persons to whom such service or labor may be due, or his, her, or their agent, or attorney, duly authorized by power of attorney, in writing, acknowledged and certified, under the Seal of some legal Officer or Court of the State or Territory in which the same may be executed, may pursue and reclaim such fugitive."—The Act goes on to provide for the enforcement of the right of reclamation, and to punish any person or persons who may interfere with, so as to hinder or prevent, the recaption of such fugitive. *U. S. Stat. at large, p.* 462.

I have already argued that the Law of seventeen hundred and ninety-three had no Constitutional force on the subject of Slavery beyond the precincts of the State and Territorial domain of the United States as defined by the treaty with Great Britain. This supplementary Act proceeds upon an admission of such limitation to the jurisdiction of the original Act and the remarks I have already made in reference to it might well be applied here. There is no protective recognition given to the ownership of Slave property in any Territory of the United States, in the Constitution: The whole extent of its protective recognition under any Compact between the Original States, limits it to the then State and Territorial domain of the United States. Its after-extension and recognition is, and always has been, and always must be, the subject of a new Compact, as I have shown in the case of the Louisiana Territory ceded by France to the United States; in the case of the admission of the State of Louisiana, in the case of the State of Missouri, of the State and Territory of Texas, and now in the case of the States and Territories comprehended, or to be comprehended, within the acquisition from Mexico.

The Compromise Measures of eighteen hundred and fifty, establishing a Territorial Government over Utah and New Mexico, admitting California into the Union, and enacting the Fugitive Slave Law, were all one political compact, made by the National Sovereignty with the people and States of the Union in relation to this newly acquired Territory, the most important parts of which related to the further extension, recognition, and protection of Slavery. It was a Compact, I repeat, outside of the Constitution; and made by a Sovereignty not known originally to the Constitution. Instead of being composed of Thirteen it was now composed of Twenty-Seven States. Five of these States were formed out of Territory which was foreign to the United States at the time the Constitution was adopted. Territory unknown to the Constitution. Territory purchased of a foreign power. Hence, the then existing National Sovereignty was not a Sovereignty created or recognized by, or deriving its Supremacy over this Territory under, the Constitution. Its acts, done in its Sovereign Capacity, must therefore be taken to be done independently of, however they may be made conformable to, the Constitution. So far then as this act of eighteen hundred and fifty, called the Fugitive Slave Law, with the other measures of this Compromise Compact, recognize or extend Slavery, or guarantee its protective recognition in any State or Territory of the United States, it is done by virtue of the New Compact and not under the Constitution. And it is unconstitutional in the same sense, and to the same extent, that the Missouri Compromise was unconstitutional. Though the act adopts the phraseology of the act of seventeen hundred and ninety-three, and speaks of persons held to labor or service in *any State or Territory* of the United States, escaping into *another State or Territory* of the United States, still these words have now a more extended meaning and reference than they had, or were designed to have, when the original act was passed. The places of ownership and escape are other and different. The places of refuge and recaption are also other and different. The Act is clearly unconstitutional, and it cannot be sustained or enforced by virtue of any authority for it derived under the Constitution; though it may be, and must be, if at all, by virtue of the Sovereign Power exercised in the "Compromise Measures" adopted as a political compact by the existing National Sovereignty in eighteen hundred and fifty.

I have thus traced the History of Slavery in the United States, in its National aspects and relations, with a view to develop and define the nature and extent of its National recognition and protection. I have endeavored to do so without any feeling of prejudice or partiality, either for or against the institution of Slavery in itself; and without any sectional animosity or partizan bias. I have shown that by and under the Constitution it was recognized in the Original States in the apportionment of taxes, in the ratio of representation in Congress, and in the guarantee of protection given to the ownership of slave property by providing for its reclamation in those States; and, by the Ordinance of seventeen hundred and eighty-seven, in the Original Territorial domain of the United States. I have shown, that beyond these limits its recognition and protection have been a matter of further compact between the States composing the National Sovereignty and the people inhabiting in the New Territory, however acquired, when it became a part of the domain of the United States, or was erected into a State and admitted into Union with the General Confederacy of

States. That even conceding that the admission of any such New State into the Union as a Slave State "on an equal footing with the Original States," guaranteed the recognition and protection of Slavery therein, in the same sense and to the same extent as in the Original States under the Constitution; it was still a restrictive recognition of it, and was based upon conditions and stipulations for its restriction which could not be violated without canceling the guarantee of recognition and protection.

I propose, now, to consider the subject under the repeal of the restriction upon Slavery contained in the Compact for the admission of Missouri into the Union as a Slave State, commonly called the Missouri Compromise.

CHAPTER III.

THE REPEAL OF THE MISSOURI COMPACT.

I.

The National Sovereignty of the United States, by compact with which the State of Missouri was created, and admitted into the Union as a Slave State, was composed, as I have said, of the Thirteen Original States; the New States of Maine, Vermont,

Illinois, Indiana, Alabama, Mississippi, Kentucky, Tennessee, and Ohio, formed out of Territory belonging to the United States, and a part of the Original States upon the adoption of the Constitution; and the State of Louisiana, formed out of a Territory subsequently purchased from France, and foreign to the domain and jurisdiction of the United States when the Constitution was adopted. This, I have observed, was a National Sovereignty different from that established by the Constitution, or contemplated in any of its provisions. No compact, therefore, for the admission of a New State framed out of such newly acquired Territory into this Confederacy, on whatever terms, could be made by virtue of any provision in the Constitution. Such compact must derive all its force and efficiency from a source outside of the Constitution, and that is, from the supremacy of this New National Sovereignty. Such, I repeat again, was the Missouri Compact; and so far as it recognized Slavery, or guaranteed protection to the ownership of Slave property by the Laws of the United States, in the State of Missouri, or in any State or Territory in the existing Confederacy which was comprehended in the provisions of the Compact; it also guaranteed the non-existence and non-extension of Slavery beyond the line of thirty-six degrees thirty minutes, North Latitude. Upon consideration of this latter guarantee it was that Missouri was admitted into the Union as a Slave State, "on an equal footing with the Original States in all respects whatever."

I have shown also, that so far as Slavery was concerned this Compact comprehended three things. 1. The National recognition of Slavery in Missouri as a State Institution. 2. The guarantee of protection to the ownership of Slave property therein, under the Laws of the United States, by giving to her and extending to the other States of the Union, the right to reclaim fugitives from service escaping into that portion of the said New Territory lying beyond thirty-six degrees thirty minutes, North Latitude. 3. It gives to Missouri the right of a representation in Congress apportioned on her Slave population.

The repeal of the Compact in relation to Slavery violated the conditions upon which all these guarantees were based, and canceled the right to them. I say, politically and as matter of law as well as of fact, it violated the condition upon which Slavery was recognized in the State of Missouri by the National Sovereignty,—upon which the protection of her citizens in the ownership of Slave property was guaranteed to them,—and upon which her representation in Congress was to be based upon her Slave population. In other words, the mutuality of the Compact was destroyed, and it became thenceforth of no further binding obligation upon the parties to it, so far at least as the recognition and protection of Slavery is concerned. Her slaves may escape into other States, or into the said Territory North of the compromise line, or into any other Territory of the United States, and where is the right to reclaim them ? It is not in the Constitution. It cannot be claimed by virtue of the broken and destroyed Compact. It is utterly gone. No law can be made or extended by Congress to enforce its reclamation in pursuance of the Constitution, for there exists no right of recaption under it. Nor can Congress pass a law to enforce it by virtue of the Compact, for that is repealed, and the laws made or extended in pursuance of it are of no legal or binding force whatever.

Conceding that her being admitted into the Union "on an equal footing with the Original States in all respects whatever," brought Missouri within the reach of the Constitutional provision guaranteeing the right of reclamation to the ownership of Slave property in the Original States, still the question recurs, what was the condition upon which she was thus admitted? Was it not the restriction, or perpetual exclusion, of Slavery from the Territory North of thirty-six degrees thirty minutes North Latitude? Was it not said, she might come into the Union as a Slave State "on an equal footing with the Original States," if she would incorporate into her State Constitution a clause prohibiting the further extension of Slavery therein, and providing for its total abolition within a given time? And the Compromise, was it not, we will agree to admit you as a Slave State "on an equal footing with the Original States in all respects whatever," if you, the people of Missouri, will unite with us, the people and States now composing the Sovereignty of the United States, in a solemn stipulation that Slavery shall be forever prohibited, or excluded, beyond a certain limit, as specified in the eighth section of the Compact? That was the condition accepted by Missouri and by the people and the States then composing the National Sovereignty. It was a condition imposed on the government of the said State and Territory for all time, by the power and Sovereignty which purchased the Territory and held supremacy over it. That condition being broken, or cancelled by the repeal of the Compact, is not the whole so far forth destroyed? Is not the privilege, or benefit, of a position in the Union "on an equal footing with the Original States," so far as Slavery is concerned, taken away? How then is the existence of Slavery, or the ownership of Slave property, in the State of Missouri, to be recognized or protected under the Constitution, or by any Law of the United States, anywhere? It cannot be.

It is evident that the Compact under which Missouri was thus admitted into the Union as a Slave State, was not a mere Congressional enactment or Law of the National Legislature, an ordinary statute repealable at will. There was a mutuality of interest and obligation in its provisions and stipulations, and in the work it wrought and was designed to accomplish, which gave to it a more permanent character and a more sacredly enduring reference. It was a Compact between the people of the Slave-holding States, and the people of the Free States then composing the National Sovereignty, with the State of Missouri, and with each other, and with the people who should thereafter inhabit in the said Territory, for the recognition and protection of Slavery on the one hand and for its restriction on the other, in Territory where it was not known to, or recognized by, the Constitution. Or, in more modern phrase, for its extension on the one side and its abolition on the other: And although it necessarily assumed the form of a Legislative enactment, as did also the Ordinance of 1787, it was nevertheless, like that Ordinance, something more than this. It was a Sovereign and National Political Compact though in form a Congressional Act: So far as it guaranteed recognition and protection to Slavery in the State of Missouri under the Constitution or by the Laws of the United States; or in any portion of the Territory which was the subject of Compact;

just so far it guaranteed its non-existence and non-extension, aye its perpetual abolition, beyond the Compromise Line.

The legal effect of the Repeal therefore was the destruction of the whole Compact in relation to Slavery. Its necessary and legitimate operation in the State of Missouri was, to cancel the guarantee of recognition and protection which it gave to Slavery and the ownership of Slave property, by the Laws of the United States.

But again, if the National recognition and protection of Slavery in Missouri is claimed under the provision of admission " on an equal footing with the Original States in all respects whatever," I ask, what was the peculiar footing on which those States stood in relation to it? The Constitution provides as to them,

ARTICLE IV. SEC. 2. "No person held to service or labor *in one State*, under the Laws thereof, escaping *into another*, shall, in consequence of any law or regulation therein, be discharged from such service or labor, but shall be delivered up on claim of the party to whom such labor or service may be due."

If this is all the recognition given to the ownership of Slave property in the State of Missouri, by virtue of her being thus admitted into the Union, it clearly does not provide for the reclamation of a fugitive escaping into any Territory of the United States. If the Territory is made a place of recaption at all, by virtue of her equality with the Original States, it can only be under the provision contained in the Ordinance of 1787, and that relates only to the Territory, or States formed out of the Territory, North-West of the River Ohio and East of the Mississippi River. I have shown that this Ordinance was adopted as to the Original States when it was made conformable to the Constitution; and thereafter again and again declared perpetual on the admission of New States, by the requisition that their Constitution should be in conformity with its provisions.

Conceding, therefore, that the Compact of admission " on an equal footing with the Original States," guaranteed the recognition of Slavery and protection to the ownership of slave property in the State of Missouri to this extent, I ask again, upon what condition ? Why on no other than the condition that that portion of Territory lying north of thirty-six degrees thirty minutes, North Latitude, and not comprehended within her proposed limits, should be forever prohibited to Slavery and consecrated irrevocably to freedom. To this the honor and good faith of the National Sovereignty, and the honor and good faith of every State then composing the Sovereignty called the United States, and of the people and State of Missouri, were solemnly and lastingly pledged.

This then is the condition, the alternative consideration, which has been violated by the Repeal. Of course the reciprocal condition is abrogated with it. Though Missouri may not thereby be deprived of her Membership in the Confederacy, yet Slavery is not recognized there, and cannot be protected there by the Laws of the United States. No law for its protective recognition can be made, as I have said before, pursuant to the Constitution. And, the Compact being repealed, its protection cannot be enforced under any law which was made, or whose provisions were extended, pursuant to the Compact.

Further, it must be observed that the Eighth Section of the Compact, which contains the Compromise, contains also the Proviso which specifies and defines the extent of the right of reclamation as guaranteed by the Compact, and that does not even mention the State of Missouri. It reads—" *Provided always*, That any person escaping into the same " (the Territory North of thirty-six degrees thirty minutes, North Latitude,) " from whom service or labor is lawfully claimed, *in any other State*, or Territory of the United States, such fugitive may be lawfully reclaimed," etc.

A strict construction of this phraseology would seem entirely to exclude " the State contemplated by this Act" from the terms of the Proviso, and to extend the right of reclaiming a fugitive slave to every other State but the proposed State of Missouri. It certainly extends the right of reclamation as to the other States beyond the Constitutional limit; and is an admission, or declaration, that it did not extend there independently of this proviso, even as regards the other and Original States, or Territory of the United States.

The Repeal of the section involves also the repeal of the Proviso, and the protective recognition, or right of reclamation therein given and guaranteed, is taken away not only from Missouri but also from every other State or Territory embraced in the provision. But of this, more hereafter.

II.

This whole work was written before the opinion of the Supreme Court was made known in the Dred Scott case. Having carefully reviewed it in connection with that opinion, I now propose to incorporate the views therein expressed by the Court, into the remainder of my argument.

I have given the case a careful examination. Every line I have written and every point I have advanced is sustained by the opinion of the Supreme Court as uttered by Chief Justice Taney in that case. In its general aspects, and in its bearing upon this subject, it is a remarkable and vastly important opinion, vastly more important for Freedom than for Slavery. Yet its import seems not to be fully comprehended either by the advocates or the opponents of Slavery extension, whether at the North or South. I thought the repeal of the Missouri Compromise was an unfortunate measure for the slave interest. I thought the Kansas-Nebraska-Act was a great bill for freedom, as great as any ever enacted by Congress, on account of this very repealing clause. I think this opinion of the Supreme Court is more so. I think when it comes to be carefully considered, it will be regarded by all parties as the most fatal blow that has ever been given to Slavery in the United States. And if persisted in in its practical applications must put an end to its further extension, perhaps to its very existence under the protective recognition of the National Sovereignty, outside of the original precincts of the United States.

The most important part of it as it applies to my argument, is the rule laid down by the Court for the construction of the Constitution. The Chief Justice—*Case p.* 32—speaking of the Constitution, says: "While it remains unaltered, it must be construed now, as it was understood at the time of its adoption. It is not only the same in words, but the same in meaning, and delegates the same powers and secures the same rights to the citizen; and as long as it continues to exist in its present form, it speaks not only the same words, but *with the same meaning and intent* with which it spoke when it came from the hands of its framers, and was voted on and adopted by the people of the United States: *any other rule of construction* would abrogate the Judicial character of this Court, and make it the mere reflex of the popular opinion or passion of the day." To all of which I have already assented.

And again, on page 38, applying this rule, he says—"The counsel for the Plaintiff has laid much stress upon that Article of the Constitution which confers on Congress the power 'to dispose of and make all needful rules and regulations respecting the Territory of the United States.'—But, in the judgment of the Court, that provision has no bearing on the present controversy, and the power there given, whatever it may be, is confined, and is intended to be confined, *to the Territory which at that time belonged to, or was claimed by*, the United States, and was *within their boundaries as settled by the Treaty with Great Britain;* and can have no influence upon a *Territory afterwards acquired from a Foreign Government.* It was a *special* provision *for a known and particular Territory*, and to meet a *present* emergency, *and nothing more.*"

And again—on page 42—in refererence to the

same provision he says—"It applied only to the property which the States *held in common at that time:* and has *no reference whatever to any Territory*, or other property, *which the New Sovereignty might afterwards itself acquire.*"—"It does not speak of *any* Territory, nor of Territories, but uses language which, according to its legitimate meaning, *points to a particular thing*. The power is given only in relation to *the* Territory of the United States, that is, *a Territory then in existence*, and *then known and claimed as the Territory* of the United States."

The rule of construction here laid down and adopted by the Court, is of course general, and is applicable to all the provisions of the Constitution in like cases. What is here said of the power of Congress in relation to the Territory of the United States, is also true of the power of Congress relative to the admission of New States formed out of it into this Union. The power to admit them is given only in relation to "a known and particular thing, then in existence, and within the then limits of the United States." It could not, by any possible intention, be supposed or construed to relate to New Territory, or New States formed out of "New Territory which the New Sovereignty might afterwards, itself, acquire of a Foreign Power," whether by purchase or by conquest. Hence, finding myself sustained by this ruling of the Supreme Court, I re-affirm that the admission of a New State formed out of such New Territory, must necessarily be a matter of compact between the people inhabiting in such Territory and the New Sovereignty, outside of the Constitution.

The same is true, also, of all the provisions of the Constitution which recognize the existence of Slavery, and protect the ownership of Slave property. They have reference to "a known and particular thing then in existence," and "within the limits of the then State and Territorial domain" of the Sovereignty called the United States. They could not, either in phraseology or intention, be supposed to relate to Slavery in Foreign Territory, or in New States formed out of Foreign Territory, "which the New Sovereignty might afterward itself acquire." For, on this subject as well as every other, as chief Justice Taney says—"The Constitution must be construed now as it was understood at the time of its adoption. It speaks not only in the same words, but with the same meaning and intent with which it spoke when it came from the hands of its framers, and was voted on and adopted by the people of the United States." The recognition of Slavery there given, and the protection it guarantees to the ownership of Slave property, "whatever it may be, is confined, and was intended to be confined to" Slavery in " the Territory which at that time belonged to, or was claimed by, the United States, and was within their boundaries as settled by the Treaty with Great Britain, and can have no relation to " Slavery in " Territory afterward acquired from a Foreign Government."

Hence I insist, that my position in relation to Slavery beyond these original precincts of the United States, is sustained by the rule of construction laid down and adopted in this decision of the Supreme Court. It is not recognized or protected beyond that limit under the Constitution. If it is recognized or protected there at all, it must be, and can only be, by virtue of the Compromise or New Compact of admission. If this Compact is pronounced void because not within the jurisdiction of the Constitution. If no valid compact on the subject of Slavery can be made outside of the Constitution by the New Sovereignty, the United States, in reference to New Territory, or States formed out of New Territory " which it has since itself acquired," then the whole theory of the extension and protective recognition of it since the adoption of the Constitution falls to the ground: Slavery gains nothing by the Missouri Compact: It gains nothing by the Compact for the annexation and admission of Texas: It gains nothing under the " Compromise Measures," or the Fugitive Slave Law of 1850.

All these Compacts, so far as they relate to Slavery, are void. All the concessions, stipulations, privileges, and agreements, which they contain in reference to it, whether express or implied, present or prospective, are void. The recognition and protection which they guarantee to it in those New States and New Territories which the New Sovereignty has since itself acquired, being outside of the original precincts of the United States, are out of the pale of the Constitution, unrecognized by its provisions, unlawful, and void. What a fell swoop is embraced in this decision! All the political advantages given to Slavery, and all the protection conceded, or sought to be conceded to the ownership of Slave property wherever it has extended itself, or seeks to extend itself, by virtue of any of these Compacts or Compromises, are, in law, void. Could anything more serviceable to freedom, or more disastrous to Slavery in the United States, be decreed by the Supreme Court?

It is not my province, nor is it my aim or my desire, to war with this decision. As a matter of opinion merely, I differ with it in some of its aspects. But as now a matter of law, the Supreme Law of the land, I look at it as such, and with a view to determine its legitimate results on this one subject of Slavery in its Constitutional relations, I commend it to the more careful and candid consideration of men of all parties in all sections of the country. In my own judgment, if carried out in its legitimate application to all Compromises on this subject, it is a death-blow to the further extension and protective recognition of Slavery in the United States. Both the Free and the Slave-holding States, both the North and the South, I confidently predict, will yet see it so:

III.

Let us look back, for one moment, and see what has been the effect of the repeal of the Missouri Compact so far as Slavery is concerned, and then couple the repeal and its effect with this decision of the Supreme Court, and we may form some idea of its ultimate legitimate tendencies in favor of freedom.

To recapitulate briefly the circumstances which originated this Compromise Compact. Missouri, a portion of the New Territory which the New Sovereignty had "itself acquired" from France after the adoption of the Constitution, applies to Congress for permission to become a State, and to be admitted into the Confederacy as such. The objection is raised, Congress has no power under the Constitution to legislate Slavery into, or to recognize by protecting its ownership in, any State or Territory of the United States beyond the limit or jurisdiction which was comprehended in its provisions at the time of its adoption. Here was a then foreign Territory however, acquired subsequently to that period. A new and very grave question is presented in relation to it, involving, as I have said, interests as sacred, and results as momentous and extensive as any which had ever agitated the Nation. Those who were instrumental in framing the Constitution had not provided for any such emergency, for the simple reason, if you please, that they had not anticipated it. They had not thought, desired, or intended, that Slavery would or should be a permanent institution among us. It had increased, however, and was rapidly extending beyond its original limits, and was covering Territory now the property of the New Sovereignty. From this New Territory, unknown to the Constitution, and "not known or claimed as the property of the United States when the Constitution was adopted," it now comes up, knocking at the doors of Congress asking that its lawful existence may be recognized, by giving it an increased representation in the national Legislature, and that its ownership may be protected by throwing around it the shield of a national Guardianship, under the laws of the United States. It was pretty generally conceded that this could not be done under a strict construction of the Constitution: No, nor even under the most liberal construction of it. Hence, in that same spirit of mutual concession and conciliation which brought about the ratification of that instrument, and in the exercise of that Sovereign right to govern which is the inseparable accompaniment of the right to acquire Territory, it was proposed to Compromise the difficulty by a new and independent compact between the States composing the New Sovereignty, and the people inhabiting in the proposed State of Missouri, and the people thereafter to inhabit in the said New Territory. By this Compact the Constitutional difficulty was waived on the one hand, and on the other, in consideration thereof, a large portion of the same New Territory, out of which the proposed State was to be erected, was consecrated irrevocably to freedom, in these words:—

"SECTION EIGHTH, RESOLVED, That in all that Territory ceded by France to the United States, under the name of Louisiana, which lies north of thirty-six degrees thirty minutes, North Latitude, not included within the limits of the State contemplated by this Act, Slavery and involuntary servitude, otherwise than in the punishment of crimes whereof the party shall have been duly convicted, *shall be, and is hereby, forever prohibited.* PROVIDED ALWAYS, That any person escaping into the same, from whom labor or service is lawfully claimed *in any other State or Territory*, in the United States, such fugitive may be lawfully reclaimed, and conveyed to the person claiming his, or her, labor or service, as aforesaid."

The Constitutional objection, therefore, which was made the basis of the Repeal, and which has been affirmed by the Supreme Court, it must be observed, was the very thing which originated the Compromise. The crisis, and the circumstances which gave birth to it, could not possibly have been met in any other or better way. There was as things then were a virtual necessity for it; otherwise Missouri could not and probably would not have been admitted into the Union as a Slave State: And every other Slave State in the Union was directly benefited by the protection guaranteed to the ownership of Slave property in the provision with reference to fugitives from service.

"The Constitution," says Chief Justice Taney again,—Dred Scot Case, page 45,—"has always been remarkable for the felicity of its arrangement of different subjects, and the perspicuity and appropriateness of the language it uses," and I may say of the clause which relates to fugitives from labor or service, as he says of the clause which relates to the power of Congress "to make all needful rules and regulations respecting the Territory, or other property, of the United States," "if that clause is construed to extend to" Slavery in "Territory acquired by the present government from a Foreign Nation outside of the limits of any charter from the British

Government to a Colony, it would be difficult to say why it was deemed necessary" to extend the right and power to reclaim a fugitive from service by this proviso in the Missouri Compact.

But this Compromise is repealed, cancelled. What then? Why the parties to the compact of which it was a part are necessarily released from all obligations whatever which it imposed upon them. While the repeal takes from Slavery all that was thereby guaranteed to it, it also restores to freedom all that it thereby gave up. While it removes the restriction put upon Slavery beyond the line of thirty-six degrees thirty minutes, North Latitude, it also withdraws the protective recognition given to it by the Proviso with reference to the fugitive escaping beyond the same line: At the same time it also opens to the entrance and occupancy of freedom, South of that line, a vast Territory from which it would have been otherwise excluded. It presents the State of Missouri as having extended and planted Slavery where she had no Constitutional right to extend it, and places her beyond the power of Congress, under the Constitution, to recognize it, or to protect her citizens in the ownership of it. It abolishes the Compact which threw the shield of a National recognition over Slavery within her own limits not only, but it also deprives her, as well as every other Slave State in the Union, of the right to reclaim fugitives from service escaping into any part of the Territory North of the Compromise line, or at least abrogates the charter which gave to the right of recaption any efficiency in law. The Repeal does all this. It does more. It has a further relation which I have before intimated, but which has not been much considered either by the friends or the opponents of the measure, and not at all by the Supreme Court. One too which has already brought into life and forceful activity a mass of influence against Slavery, which mere opposition to the institution as such could not of itself have originated.

There is, and there always has been, in the minds of a large portion, if not all of the people of the Free States, a difficulty on the subject of these Compacts, which does not touch the question of the right or the wrong of holding human beings in involuntary servitude, or Slavery. That is—the right of representation in Congress apportioned on a Slave population in the Slave-holding States. If, say they, human beings are to be treated as property for the purpose of holding them in bondage, why treat them as persons for the mere sake of increasing the power of Slave owners to extend and perpetuate Slavery? If the claim of representation is based upon their character as property, why not establish a similar basis of representation on property in the Free States? If, on the other hand, it is based on their character as persons, as human beings susceptible of acquiring rights, and holding interests in the body politic which may be the subject of Legislation, why not treat them as such and give them the right to choose their own representatives? Where, say they, is the law of right, or justice, or equity, upon which this ratio of representation is conceded to Slave States formed out of New Territory "acquired by the New Sovereignty since the adoption of the Constitution?" I answer them, nowhere, unless it is the creation of the Compromise or Compact of admission. It must originate in the "equal footing with the Original States in all respects whatever," provided and guaranteed by that Compact. In this it does originate, and by this it must be limited and defined. It is the Compact that gives to Slavery a legal recognition within the limits of the States which were parties to it, and the New State created by it, which it had not and could not have under the Constitution. The Constitution confers no powers upon Congress which authorized or warranted it. The advocates of the Repeal, both in and out of Congress, insisted upon this. The Supreme Court have so decided. Therefore, whatever recognition is given to Slavery under the New Compact, must derive all its efficiency from the exercise of that Sovereign power to govern incident to the Sovereign power to acquire New Territory, independently of the Constitution. There must be a New Compact outside of the Constitution, even if it can only be made by a Compromise. Hence the irresistible conclusion, that Slavery has been extended, exists, has rights, is recognized and protected, beyond the limits of the original Constitutional jurisdiction of the United States, only by virtue of enactments of Congress brought into existence under political compacts between the Free and the Slave States composing the then existing Sovereignty, and the State created and admitted into the Union under such Compact.

These Ordinances or enactments involving a mutuality of obligation, and containing specific stipulations and conditions in relation to Slavery, are in the nature of irrevocable political compacts between all of the States of the Union, under whose general sovereignty the guarantee of its recognition in the New State "on the same footing as in the Original States" is established. The Repeal of any one of these Compacts, or Ordinances, weakens the obligation which upholds all the rest. The judgment of the Supreme Court pronouncing them unconstitutional, and therefore of no binding force in relation to Slavery, cancels that obligation.

The repeal and the decision, therefore, combine to take from the institution of Slavery not only the legal protection it acquired by the Compact, but also all the advantages it gained by being thereby placed "on an equal footing with" Slavery in "the Original States," among which by far the most important was and is the right of representation based on a Slave population. They do more, they give to the people of the Free States a right to insist that Slavery shall no longer be recognized, or the ownership of Slave property protected by the general government, where it has been established or extended, or proposes to be, by virtue of any of these Compacts. This ratio of representation based on a slave population, originally inherent and peculiar only in the Original States, falls to the ground in the State of Missouri. The same is true of Slavery in every other State where it has been, or shall be, permitted to plant itself independently of the Constitution, and wherever it is recognized and protected under the Laws of the United States in pursuance of any such Compromise or Compact; the Supreme Court also itself being judge.

IV.

It was in these aspects of it that the Repeal of the Missouri Compact in 1854, originated and combined a power against Slavery in the United States which was all but irresistible. Theretofore the existence of Slavery among us had been disturbed, never really or effectively threatened or endangered, by men calling themselves "Abolitionists," "Anti-Slavery Men,"

"Liberty-Men," "Free-Soilers," etc. No two of these parties had ever been able to unite with each other for any efficient purpose. Each held opinions and principles in other respects divers from the rest. And therefore each measurably weakened or counteracted the ability of the other to accomplish anything against Slavery. Besides this antagonism between themselves, their aims were more powerfully hindered by the great body of men in the Free States, who felt bound to sustain these Compromise Compacts irrespective of their own private opinions on the subject of Slavery. The operation of this Repeal, therefore, ignoring as it did the binding force of the Compromises, or the principle which gave them their binding force, was to unite all these discordant factions and the more conservative opponents of Slavery in one "party of opposition" to its further progress, and if need be to its actual existence. Many of them never loved it and rejoiced at heart in the removal of those obligations which smothered and fettered their repugnance to it. Many more came up to the conflict against it, inflamed by an honest indignation at so ruthless a violation of so solemn a Compact. Some did it from principle, some from motives of resentment, and some with political aims; while all seemed to feel that the moral sense of every well-instructed mind in the community, yea of the whole civilized world, was with them.

But this fearful flame even, gathered fresh fuel from the singular inconsistency of the advocates of Slavery. While repealing one Compromise and abandoning the principle which alone secured protection to the owership of Slave property escaping into the New Territory acquired by the New Sovereignty after the Constitution was adopted; they enforce its protection under a precisely similar Compromise, made to accomplish a similar object in such New Territory, viz., under the Fugitive Slave Law of 1850. This Law as I have shown was the creation of a Compromise no more and no less sacred or obligatory than the Missouri Compact. Then, for the first time in my life, I trembled for our National Union. I wrote to a Southern friend, under date May twenty-second, 1854, as follows:

"I have said that the Repeal of the Missouri Compromise is fatal to Slavery, and gave you the reasons for my opinion. But simultaneously with this repeal I hear that the Fugitive Slave Law of 1850—the creation of a similar compromise—is being enforced in favor of Slavery in Boston. I am more than ever confident in my judgment of the effect and operation of that repeal. The Repeal itself, I have claimed, is fatal to the Slave interest. It is made more surely so by this hot and inconsistent haste of Slavery to clutch her victim. Better to have lost a thousand slaves than to have done this. The crisis reveals how much of human sympathy one human being doomed to involuntary servitude can awaken; and if one, how much more the thousands which, in the minds of our Northern demagogues and fanatics at least, now groan under the scourge and the lash?

"But, my friend, this fugitive,—mark me,—this fugitive will be delivered up. Accept, slaveholder, your trembling captive.

'The Law allows it, the Court awards it.'

"We are a law-loving and a law-abiding people. In this you did well, to accept it as a guarantee for the safety of your property even in human flesh and bones, as well as of your own personal protection. Let the example teach you in like manner to respect the Law, should it hereafter exercise itself in protecting such as it now delivers over to your arbitrary will. But, before you go, permit me to say to you, that you have made a fearful experiment. A people innately and by education hostile to Slavery, goaded almost to madness in their rage at such an exhibition of it, and restrained from a violent outburst of passion only by the might and the majesty of the Law, is a hazardous encounter for you to have ventured upon at such a time as this, and may well make you, even while triumphant, tremble. For from the terrific restraint thus imposed by the Law who can calculate the re-bound, when this same people turn and look upon Slavery where the Law which protected it is taken away. And if you persist in it of this you may rest assured, that the Laws which now recognize or protect it outside of the Constitution will soon be written down—*rasa tabula.*

"I see it and hear it everywhere I turn. The merchant forgets his business, the artizan his trade, the mechanic his shop, the laborer his tools, the operative his work, and eyen the politician his partizanship, and all unite in denouncing Slavery. The looker-on may at once see that something vital is at stake. That there is something more than ordinarily powerful agitating the deeper feelings of the community. It agitates the pulpit, the bench, the bar, and our Halls of Legislation. Men who never before held parley with their fellows on the subject of Slavery, now agitate it, denounce it, and swear interminable war against it. Shrewd politicians begin to make hostility to it a basis for calculating their own chances for future elevation. Commercial men and editors of newspapers, in our seaboard and inland cities, are estimating in dollars and cents their interest in the agitation. Land-speculators are sending forward their agents to secure for the more profitable occupancy of freedom, the yet unvisited soil so wrongfully thrown open to the hostile occupancy of Slavery. The more bitter and subtle enemies of Slavery have already surveyed the most desirable and expeditious route to this virgin Territory for their 'Underground Rail Road,' and we almost hear the shout of its passengers mingling with the thunder of its cars, as they are borne on to the home of freedom. The tread of her more orderly and disciplined armies sounds grateful in the ears of the oppressed, and the noise of the clanking chains as they fall from the unfettered limbs of the bond-man, is hushed amid the exulting and jubilant pœans of the free.

"As for myself, my friend, you know I am not, and never was an "Abolitionist," or an "Anti-Slavery-Man," or a "Free-Soiler." I was educated in the old fashioned

Protestant dogma that "The Bible is the only rule of Faith to man," and I retain enough of that venerable notion to decline sitting in judgment over my fellow-man as to the right or the wrong of holding human beings in bondage. I have, moreover, been among Slavery and have seen it in all its aspects and conditions, and I confess to an entire softening down of my prejudices against it. But were I the most inveterate and determined abolitionist in the world—aside from the violation of plighted faith which it involves—I would rejoice in the repeal of the Missouri Compromise. I would rejoice in it, not only on account of the source whence it originated, but also and more for the perfect looseness with which it throws open the Slavery agitation without any fault or agency of ours. And I should regard it as a demonstration of the presence of that Providence who 'maketh the wrath of man to praise him,' while 'the' unprofitable 'remainder of that wrath He restrains.'"

Such were the views which I entertained of the Repeal in 1854. I saw a dark cloud gathering in the horizon. I watched it anxiously as it grew blacker, rose higher, and finally encircled the political firmament. I saw the people and parties of the Free States combining together under skillful demagogues and politicians in a party of "Opposition to Slavery," with a watchword created by this Repeal—"Freedom for Kansas." The plausible and shrewdly devised theory under which all the discordant elements of faction in the Free States were thus brought to unite, was—not as "Abolitionists," not as "Free-Soilers," not as "Liberty-men," nor yet even as "Northern-men," but—as "lovers of truth, justice, humanity and freedom:"—and who that beheld it from without did not tremble at the reach and the fury of the political tornado their union created?

V.

Such was the effect of the Repeal of the Compromise by virtue of which the Territory of Missouri was erected into a State Organization, and admitted into the Union as a Slave State, "on an equal footing with the Original States in all respects whatever." The Combination which it originated against Slavery was composed of the most divers, radical, destructive and discordant elements ever cast into the political alembick of any nation. Out of it was engendered the most fearful development of sectional animosity this country has ever known: And the utter overthrow of the Confederacy, I religiously believe, was averted only by the interposition of that Providence who has ever guided and controlled our National destiny.

Yet in all honesty it must be admitted that the claim of "Freedom for Kansas" is not all "fiction," or "humbug." It is founded in the eternal principles of right between man and man. Politically, legally, so far I mean as the decision of the question is under the control of Congress, or the National Sovereignty, the opponents of Slavery-Extension have a right to claim it. A right founded in honor, honesty and justice. A right guaranteed to them, and to humanity, and to the people who may inhabit in that Territory, by as solemn and enduring a Compact as any the National Sovereignty ever made with the people and the States of the Union. I do not wonder they made so much of it in our recent Presidential Canvass. The Repeal outraged justice and insulted freedom; and were it not for the more recent decision of the Supreme Court pronouncing the Compact itself illegal and void, I would insist, not as a partizan or a sectionalist, but as mere matter of law, that Congress has no power or right to admit Kansas into the Union as a Slave State. Certainly under the Missouri Compact it has no more right to do it than it would have had to admit Michigan, Indiana, or Ohio, as Slave States, in defiance of the political compact contained in the Ordinance of 1787. Indeed, the compact being repealed, what right has Congress under the Constitution at all to extend by recognizing or protecting Slavery in any State or Territory North of thirty-six degrees thirty minutes, North Latitude? In any Territory acquired by the New and Enlarged Sovereignty, since the adoption of the Constitution, from a Foreign power? Assuredly none. The Supreme Court says none. It cannot do it unless by virtue of a New Compact, a New Compromise. But what availeth either under the Constitution if tested by the opinion of the Supreme Court? Whatever Kansas might do in her own capacity as a State Sovereignty in relation to Slavery, in case of her actual admission into the Union as such, Congress is evidently without power under the Constitution to recognize its extension, or to protect its establishment within her precincts.

"It seems however to be supposed," says the Chief Justice—Dred Scott Case, page 57—"that there is a difference between property in a Slave and other property, and that different rules may be applied to it in expounding the Constitution of the United States—and *if* the Constitution recognizes the right of property of the master in a Slave, and makes no distinction between that description of property and other property owned by a citizen, no tribunal, acting under the authority of the United States, whether it be legislative, executive, or judicial, has a right to draw such a distinction, or to deny to it the benefit of the provisions and guarantees which have been provided for the protection of private property against the encroachments of the government."

This, I concede, may all be very true as applied to Slave property within the limits of the original precincts of the United States. But the Constitution itself did not recognize "the right of property of a master in a Slave" beyond the original limits of its own jurisdiction. It did make a distinction between that species of property owned within, and that owned outside of, the then Territorial precincts of the United States. Under the authority of the Constitution Congress prohibited the exportation of Slaves from the United States into foreign Territory, as also their importation into the United States from such Territory; and I see no reason why it should have less power over it, or sink the distinction in the same Territory, after it becomes the property of the United States.

It seems, moreover, that "different rules" have been applied by the Government of the United States to property in a Slave, from those which obtain in relation to "other property." It seems to me that the application of the whole power of the National Sovereignty, both civil and military, to enforce the recaption of a Fugitive Slave is "a different rule" from any which relates to "other property." I am also inclined to think that the rule of representation in Congress which bases it on a Slave population, is "a different rule" from any that is applied to "other property," and might well be taken to aid our construction of the Constitution in relation to it. But I do not mean to controvert the ruling of the Supreme Court. I will concede that there is no "distinction between property in a slave and other property," and that "different rules" may not be applied to it "in expounding the Constitution." Let us then apply the same rule which is applied by the Court itself. It says—Dred Scott Case, p. 42—that the power given to Congress by the Constitution "to dispose of and make all needful rules and regulations respecting the Territory of the United States, applies only to *property* which the States held in common *at that time*, and had *no reference whatever* to any Territory, *or other property*, which the New Sovereignty might afterward itself acquire." And—Ibid, pages 47, 48—"whether we take the particular clause in question, by itself, or in connection with the other provisions of the Constitution, we think it clear, that it applies only to the particular Territory of which we have spoken, and cannot *by any just rule of interpretation*, be extended to Territory which the New Government might afterward obtain from a foreign nation." Consequently the power to prohibit Slavery "which Congress may have lawfully exercised in this" (the Original) "Territory, while it remained under a Territorial Government, and which may have been sanctioned by judicial decision, can furnish no justification and no argument to support a similar exercise of power over Territory afterward acquired by the Federal Government. We put aside, therefore, any argument, drawn from precedents, showing the extent of the power which the General Government exercised over Slavery in this" (Original) "Territory, as altogether inapplicable to the case before us:" viz. the prohibition of Slavery in this newly acquired Territory.

Now if this be so, how, I ask, can any provision in the Constitution in relation to Slavery "as it existed at that time," and in the original precincts of the United States, have any wider reference than the provision above alluded to by the Court? How can the right of reclamation given by the Constitution, be extended to "other property" in slaves, in other and then alien Territory, "which the New Sovereignty might afterward itself acquire?" Or, how can the provision of the Constitution in relation to the admission of New States, be extended to States formed out of "New Territory which the New Sovereignty might afterward itself acquire?" Or where, under this rule of construction, does the New Sovereignty itself derive its power to admit New States; or "to make all needful rules and regulations" respecting this new foreign Territory, or "other property" therein? I admit, and my argument is, that it does not derive these powers originally from the Constitution; and I have already pointed out the source whence they emanate, but will here let the Supreme Court itself answer the question.

In the case of the American Ocean Insurance

Company, referred to by Chief Justice Taney,—Dred Scott Case, pages 48, 49—the Court before whom that case was tried is cited as saying—"Perhaps the power of governing a Territory belonging to the United States which has not, by becoming a State, acquired the means of self government, may result necessarily, from the facts, that it is not within the jurisdiction of any particular State, and is within the power and jurisdiction of the United States. The right to govern, may be the inevitable consequence of the right to acquire Territory."—"The Power," adds the Chief Justice, "stands firmly on the latter alternative put by the Court—that is, *as the inevitable consequence of the right to acquire Territory.*"

That is it, precisely as I have contended. The Court here recognizes the distinction between the power of the National Sovereignty derived under the Constitution, and that derived outside of the Constitution. The power to govern thus originated then, is acquired, as I have said, independently of the Constitution :—and it is absolutely Sovereign, and exclusive. But, again, whence the power to acquire Territory? It is not given by the Constitution, "except,"—as Chief Justice Taney says, Dred Scott case, page 52—"by the admission of New States:" And I have shown that it cannot be derived, under that provision in the Constitution, according to the rule of construction laid down and adopted by the

Supreme Court, that is, "*by any just rule of interpretation*, according to its original meaning and intent," except within the limits of its jurisdiction, "as understood when it first came from the hands of its framers, and was voted on and adopted by the people of the United States—viz.:—within their boundaries as settled by the Treaty with Great Britain," in 1783.

All this language is direct, "positive, precise, and determinate." It is the voice of the highest tribunal in our land. The voice of Supremacy itself. The voice of Constitutional Supremacy. It speaks to the point, and in tones of authority which have already reverberated throughout the civilized world. It tells us that the National Sovereignty has no power, under the Constitution, to acquire foreign Territory, or to govern it when acquired. That its power to acquire Territory originates in its inherent Sovereignty outside of the Constitution: And this Sovereign right to acquire,—it tells us also—is the only source of its Sovereign right to govern such "Territory, or other property."

Now I submit, if this Sovereignty may be thus exercised independently of the Constitution, in relation to the acquisition of New Territory, or other property; why may it not also exercise itself in the same way in relation to other Slave property, coming under its jurisdiction in consequence of this new acquisition of Territory ? If it may derive power over the new Territory, independently of the Constitution, why may it not also over Slavery in such Territory ? It certainly must. Why then may it not prohibit as well as protect or recognize it therein ? As I have before observed, it prohibited the exportation of Slaves from the United States into such Territory, and the importation of Slaves into the United States from such Territory, before it made the purchase ; and may it not do the same thing afterward ? Certainly it may. It did it then by virtue of the Constitutional power it had over it. It may do it now by virtue of its Sovereignty over it, outside of the Constitution. Otherwise its jurisdiction over Slavery in foreign Territory, is greater than its power over it in its own National domain, which will hardly be seriously claimed. *Sec.* 2, *U. S. Stat. at large*, 426.

Hence, again, I conclude that the Missouri Compact was not a mere legal enactment of the National Legislative, made in pursuance of any authority derived under the Constitution. But that it was an exercise of the Sovereign capacity of the New Sovereignty exercising itself in forming a political Compact in reference to matters entirely within the scope of its jurisdiction, independently of the Constitution. So also was the Compact for the Annexation and admission of Texas. So also the Compact of the

"Compromise measures," embracing the Protective Slave Law of 1850. These Compacts severally and respectively contain the only true guarantee of the National recognition of Slavery, and of protection in the ownership of Slave property, beyond the original Constitutional limits of the United States. And hence the importance of upholding and preserving them in their original perpetuity and integrity; far more important to Slavery than to freedom.

VI.

I have thus traced the history of the National recognition and relations of Slavery, from the establishment of the Confederacy to the present time.

I have pointed out the nature and extent of the National recognition given to it under the Constitution. I have also pointed out the origin and true guarantee of its protective recognition beyond that limit. I think I have sufficiently elucidated and demonstrated my position. The Opinion of the Supreme Court of the United States in the Dred Scott Case substantiates it. If I understand that opinion, it decides, as matter of National Law, that the Government of the United States cannot make a Compact, under the Constitution, for the prohibition of Slavery in Territory which it may have acquired from a Foreign power since its adoption. That is, under the Constitution, it cannot prohibit the Slave owner from carrying his property into such New Territory after it becomes the property of the United States, although it might do so, and actually did do so, before it became the property of the United States. I can easily understand how this might be claimed under the Constitution with reference to Territory originally a part of the precincts of the United States, although such claim might be rebutted, in part at least, by the Ordinance of 1787. But to say that the exportation of a Slave into Foreign Territory to day, is the Slave Trade, and justly prohibited by the laws of the United States under the Constitution: And that to-mor row the transportation of the same Slave, into the same Territory become the property of the United States, cannot be prohibited by the Sovereignty which has purchased it, outside of the Constitution, is what I cannot understand, and what I do not think the Supreme Court means to say. I am satisfied that the Court was speaking only of the power of Congress under the Constitution. And in that view I coincide with it.

If however, the New Sovereignty may not, under the Constitution, prohibit the entrance of Slavery into such New Territory after it has become the property of the United States, can it recognize and protect it there under the Constitution ? Can it legislate it into such New Territory under the Constitution? Certainly not: But it may do all this by virtue of its Sovereignty over it outside of the Constitution. The Sovereign right to acquire Territory involves the Sovereign right to govern it: And if the right to govern is Sovereign, independently of the Constitution, it may, by virtue thereof, protect or prohibit Slavery therein; the Supreme Court itself being Judge.

I have said thàt the Repeal of the Missouri Com pact, combined with the ruling of the Supreme Court, is fatal to Slavery in the United States. I say it, because, as I have shown, the same reasoning will overthrow the other Compromises relating to it in the Territory acquired from Texas and from Mexico. Because, the ruling of the Court must also prevail in all future legislation by Congress with reference to it, and in the action of the government in reference to it, in Territory which has been, or which may hereafter be, acquired from a foreign power. And it cannot be otherwise than fatal to Slavery. If there is no power to prohibit it there, neither is there any power to protect it there, under the Constitution. There is no escape from it unless you admit a Supremacy over this New Territory, existing in the National Sovereignty outside of the Constitution. I say this in no partizan or sectional spirit. I have not written with any such spirit, or with any such motives or aims. I hope our brethren of the Slave-holding States will look at it in the same spirit, and with like candor and fairness, and that they will hold on righteously to the remedy. That is, that they will sustain these Compromises as the Ordinances of a competent National Sovereignty derived outside of the Constitution. They must do it. It is for their interest to do it. Freedom can well afford to see these Compacts discarded and their mutuality destroyed. But Slavery cannot. Yet such an issue should be deprecated and averted as a dire calamity both to freedom and to humanity. Let the guarantee of prohibition contained in the Missouri Compromise be faithfully carried out, as it was in the North-West Territory under the Ordinance of 1787, and all may yet be well. Agitation will cease, harmony will be again restored, and sectionalism will be disrobed of its power. But provoke a sectional, or partizan, or even a legitimate application of this ruling of the Supreme Court to all existing and future Compromises on the subject of Slavery, and you annihilate forever the recognition and protection given to it, outside of the original precincts of the United States, by the guarantee of admission into the Union "on an equal footing with the Original States in all respects whatever." And when you provoke such a conflict as this you lessen the political power and shorten the duration of Slavery, by depriving it of a National guardianship under the Government and Laws of the United States. The result possibly might be the destruction of our National Union. And is the bondage, or the redemption, of three millions of negro slaves worth such a cost?

My fellow-countrymen, both of the North and the South, both of the Free and the Slave States, let us look at this matter as our forefathers looked at it, with an enlarged patriotism, with a comprehensive philanthropy. Let us plant ourselves firmly and unitedly on this common and conservative ground of the supremacy of our National Sovereignty in its own Territory, and the validity of the political Ordinances made by it on this subject of Slavery therein. Slavery must continue to be a part of our political existence for many years yet to come. God only knows how long, or how variously, it may be interwoven with our National Destiny. New Territory will again be acquired by this New Sovereignty, and New States formed out of it will continue to seek admission into our National Confederacy. Other Sovereignties it may be, now independent, and other dependent Colonies, may also ask to be annexed to these United States. With some of them will and must come a new and additional Slave population which will again call for the action of our National Government in relation to it. It will call for new Compacts, for new concessions and restrictions, for new guards and guarantees. If its recognition be but limited to an already existing slave population with its natural increase as the only source of supply, let it come. For freedom's sake, for humanity's sake I say, let it come. Be it ours to stand fast upon the Constitutional limit to its National recognition. Beyond that let us hold it to a stern and strict fulfillment of the conditions of the political compact made for its further extension. Let us exercise in regard to it a patriotic concession, without any timid or time-serving submission; a wise and just conciliation, without any servile fear or ungenerous compulsion. Thus may we preserve and perpetuate this Union as the greatest political good of which we are made the conservators. Thus may we best contribute to fulfill the mission of this Mighty Republic to mankind. For my own part, although I would oppose with a resolute resistance the aggressive progress of Slavery over broken Compacts and discarded Compromises, yet if it be but restricted as I have supposed, I would that it might go, and be recognized, and its ownership protected by the National Sovereignty, in every State and Territory in the United States, rather than that this Union itself should be dissolved. Better, far better, that the whole slave population now existing on or near this continent should be brought under our restrictive *jurisdiction and Laws, and

* It was stated by Mr. Buxton in a recent debate in the British House of Commons on the subject—that "there has been of late years a

under the ameliorating influences of a Protestant Christian ownership and servitude, than that this Union should be dissolved. For what hope I ask, what hope is there for freedom, what hope for humanity, in the dissolution of our National Union? When, in the history of any nation, has so much been done for freedom and for humanity as when the American Colonies united under the martial manifesto to resist the aggressions of the Parent State? When so much, as when they united in the Declaration of Independence and proclaimed themselves absolved from all allegiance to its oppressive Sovereignty? When so much, as when they made that Union perpetual under the Confederation and thereby compelled the recognition of their Independence? When so much, as when having secured that Independence they united under the more perfect and enduring compact of the present Constitution? Was nothing gained for freedom then? Nothing for humanity? Was it nothing, for this new Sovereignty as it took its place proudly among the Nations of the Earth, to proclaim its hostility to involuntary

decided increase in the Slave Trade between the Spanish Colony of Cuba and the coast of Africa. In 1847 there were only one thousand slaves imported into Cuba, whereas during the last two years the number had averaged about twenty thousand."—*London Daily Times, Jan.*, 1858.

Let Cuba become a part of the United States and this source of supply is cut off.

servitude and oppression by prohibiting the Slave Trade? Who shall undertake to say how many thousand generations of Africans, to the remotest posterity, were saved from Slavery by that one great Act of Emancipation? Was it nothing, to shut off from the Slave Trade that extensive country purchased from France, the Louisiana Territory? Nothing to bring its existing mass of servitude, its ports, and its commerce, under the prohibitions, restrictions, and penalties, of the Laws of the United States in relation to Slavery? Has nothing been done for freedom, or for humanity, by restricting the source of supply over this vast continent to the natural increase of an already existing slave population? Nothing, in the redemption of New-Mexico, Utah, and California, from Mexican misrule and Romish superstition? Nothing, in closing the ports of the Atlantic, of Florida, of the Gulf of Mexico, and of the vast Pacific coast, against the traffic in human flesh and bones? When or where, in the history of any people, has the area of freedom been so munificently extended and guarded as by these United States of America? Look at the New Republic rising, already risen on the shores of Africa, Liberia, a bow of promise and of hope to the Ethiopian tribes, the work of the United States.—Is that nothing to freedom? Nothing to humanity? And can human wisdom or forethought calculate the value to mankind, of a Confederacy which in less than three quarters of a century has done so much for our race? Oh ye who at heart love freedom, ye who at heart love humanity, cease to revile a Union of States which has done, and is doing, so much for both. Cease to talk of the dissolution of a Republic whose existence is so necessary to the freedom and the welfare of the down-trodden children of men.

Cease to talk of the instant emancipation, or the perpetual bondage, of three millions of negro slaves, as a greater good to mankind than the existence under this Federal Union of twenty-three millions of white men, with all their silver and their gold; their institutions of government, of learning, of religion, of freedom, of humanity, of philanthropy, and of charity; their enterprizes of commerce, of exploration, of art, and of science; so munificently employed in ameliorating the condition of our race all over the world. The Union—in all its aspects and relations whether of Freedom or of Slavery—The Union is of God. "Ye cannot overthrow it, lest haply ye be found even to fight against God."

THE END.